M000169703

SHEPHERDS
OF THE FLOCK

SHEPHERDS
OF THE FLOCK

Elevating Home and Visiting Teachers to
Home Ministers

written by
STEPHEN N. WEBBER

Copyright © 2015, Stephen N. Webber
www.shepherdsoftheflock.com

© 2015 Stephen N. Webber

All Rights Reserved. No part of this book may be reproduced in any form whatsoever, whether by graphic, visual, electronic, film, microfilm, tape recording, or any other means, without prior written permission of the author, except in the case of brief passages embodied in critical reviews and articles. This book is not an official publication of The Church of Jesus Christ of Latter-day Saints. The views expressed herein are the responsibility of the author and do not necessarily represent the position of the Church.

ISBN: 978-0-578-18061-8

Published and Distributed by Timpanogos Media, LLC
Imprint of Timpanogos Media, LLC
4627 West 9850 North
Cedar Hills, UT 84062
801-369-3029
www.timpmedia.com
www.shepherdsoftheflock.com

Cover design by Stephen N. Webber
Cover design © 2016 Stephen N. Webber

ISBN: 978-0-578-18061-8 (paperbound)

First Printing: May 2016
V7OCT2016
Printed in the United States of America

To my amazing children
Janae, Kathryn, Madison, Quincy & Harrison

Contents

Acknowledgments

As is the case in any major accomplishment, there are usually several people behind the scenes who are instrumental in helping make it a success, especially one as difficult as writing a book for the first time.

Accordingly, there have been many people who have helped make this book great by sharing their wisdom, experience and examples. Some friends have provided me with inspiration for characters, and others have directed me to meaningful quotes or scriptures that I have used. There are however, five very important contributors who need to be acknowledged:

Brady Giles, my first home teaching companion, taught me by example what a true shepherd is supposed to do. He showed me how home teaching can change lives and build eternal friendships.

Jeff Call, a very successful writer and sports columnist, and one of my counselors when I served as bishop, was kindly-critical of my first effort on this book. He encouraged me to step out of the box and write about home teaching with the same passion and enthusiasm that I would speak about it from the pulpit. His wise and honest counsel helped me find the proper tone and tempo, resulting in a book about home and visiting teaching that is actually fun, interesting and hard to put down.

Kevin Doman, the real-life mission president's assistant in Chapter 10, taught me over 30 years ago that selfless service is the gateway to Christlike love. The timely testimony he shared with me as a young missionary turned out to be one of the most important lessons of my life.

Kathryn Webber Burton, my daughter, volunteered to be the formal editor of *Shepherds of the Flock*. As we reviewed this book together multiple times—out loud—she added scores of vital improvements and corrections to my improper spelling, punctuation and grammar. She also provided reassuring confirmation along the way that the principles covered in this book are true. It was fun to work together with Katie on this project, but it was also an honor and privilege to have her want to participate in such a collaborative way.

Most importantly, I want to express my appreciation to my eternal companion and partner, Jana. She has given me the ultimate pattern of Christlike service to follow and emulate throughout our marriage. I am so grateful for her example of lovingly visiting and ministering to dozens of women over the years. She truly understands and embraces the Lord's mandate to feed His sheep.

Introduction

*"Home teaching is one of our most urgent and most
rewarding opportunities to nurture and inspire, to counsel
and direct our Father's children. ... It is a divine service, a
divine call. It is our duty as Home Teachers to carry the
divine spirit into every home and heart. To love the work
and do our best will bring unbounded peace, joy, and
satisfaction to a noble, dedicated teacher of God's children."[1]
President David O. McKay*

As a former young mens president, elders quorum president,
high priest group leader and bishop, I have seen the difference
that valiant home and visiting teaching can make in a ward, in a
family, and in the individual performing the service. Effective
home ministering can strengthen faith, change lives, and bring
souls unto Christ. I believe that Elder Jeffrey R. Holland's recent
message to become "God's emissaries to His children" and "to
love and care and pray for the people you are assigned to"[2] is a
timely mandate to each member of the Church of Jesus Christ
of Latter-day Saints to bear one another's burdens and minister
to each other's needs.

Though initially prompted to write a book about home
teaching over 10 years ago, I resisted taking on the project. I felt

---

1 Quoted by Marion G. Romney, in Conference Report, 8 Apr. 1966, p. 7

2 In Conference Report, Oct. 2016, *Emissaries to the Church*, Elder Jeffrey R.
Holland

that people would be reluctant to read a book about the most procrastinated responsibility in the Church. But over the years, I have come to realize that many members do not have a testimony of home and visiting teaching, simply because they have never been properly instructed about the actual purpose or process of ministering to the families in their ward.

For years, home and visiting teachers have been encouraged to visit their assigned families each month, share a brief message from a Church magazine, and then report back that the families have been visited. Though this is what they were taught to do, it is not what the Lord actually wants them to do.

Shepherds of the Flock - Elevating Home and Visiting Teachers to Home Ministers shines a bright light on an important doctrine and principle that has been overlooked and underemphasized for a long time. The object of this book is to inspire and help readers understand the true purpose of the home and visiting teaching programs, and see that their assignment has the potential to be so much more than a ten minute lesson from a Church magazine.

Home and visiting teaching is divinely designed to help the bishop assess and minister to the needs of each family, and it all starts with Ammon-like shepherds that will feed and protect the flock. The Lord wants dedicated, courageous and loving shepherds—not lukewarm hirelings.

To accomplish this task in the most interesting and entertaining way, this book has been written in the format of a novel from the perspective of a newly called bishop. However, it is vital to understand that this is not a bishop's training guide. This unique vantage point effectively demonstrates—to all home and visiting teachers—how magnifying their assignments can affect their entire ward, not just their assigned families. The reader is given a floor-to-ceiling description of the shepherding process, including the responsibilities of their leaders as they receive and act upon information concerning the welfare of each family in the ward. *Shepherds of the Flock* delivers a clear picture of the full potential of this inspired program when administered properly and helps the reader clearly see why President Ezra Taft Benson called it the *"greatest calling in the Church."*

Keep in mind, home teaching is different from visiting teaching—as it is a priesthood duty—much like missionary service is for all worthy and able young men. The Handbook allows for variations in the two programs, and as a result, they are not entirely interchangeable. However, most of the principles in this book concerning ministering undoubtedly apply to both home and visiting teaching.

As you prayerfully read and apply the principles taught in *Shepherds of the Flock*, you will find new ways to improve your own home and visiting teaching, and in turn find renewed meaning and joy as you serve your assigned families. As you accept and magnify your calling to feed the sheep of the Good Shepherd, you are helping Him accomplish His work and His glory in a very literal way. As a consequence, He will bless you with the gift of charity, and unlimited inspiration for those to whom you minister.

Chapter 1

The Call

"So long as life lasts, and so long as we possess ability to do
good, to labor for the upbuilding of Zion and for the benefit
of the human family, we ought, with willingness, to yield
with alacrity to the requirements made of us
to do our duty, little or great."[3]
President Joseph F. Smith

It was a beautiful summer evening, and Brother Stephens and his son John had just returned from home teaching the Anderson family. They were enjoying their time together and laughing about something John had just said, when they walked through the front door.

"Mom, we're home," yelled John.

The house was unusually quiet.

"Honey?" Brother Stephens walked into the front room where he found his wife waiting for them on the couch. She had the phone in her hand and a very nervous look on her face. She looked almost pale, and immediately Brother Stephens could tell that something wasn't right.

Brother Stephens looked at John, nodded his head toward the kitchen, and said quietly, "Son, give us a minute."

---

[3] In Conference Report, Apr. 1914, p. 7, President Joseph F. Smith

With a concerned look on his face, John slowly backed out of the room, until he disappeared into the kitchen.

When Brother Stephens heard the refrigerator door open, and knew John was more interested in grabbing a snack than listening to his parents, he anxiously asked his wife, "What's wrong?"

Sister Stephens looked at him and said, "The stake president wants to talk with you next Sunday."

He relaxed a bit and said, "Is that all? By the look on your face, I thought there had been a terrible accident or something."

She looked at him and then said, "He wants me to come with you."

Brother Stephens slowly sat down next to her on the sofa. "Well, that can't be good," he muttered as they sat together holding hands, each one lost in their own thoughts.

Chapter 2

The Load

"We praise and honor these worthy shepherds of the flock, judges in Israel, leaders and teachers of the people, men who love and are loved by those whom they serve as under-shepherds of the Lord Jesus Christ. God bless these good men! And God bless their faithful wives, whose loyalty and support make their service possible."[4]
Elder Dallin H. Oaks

Brother and Sister Stephens sat silently in their car in the church parking lot after their meeting with the stake president. Several minutes passed before either of them could articulate their thoughts. Prior to the appointment, when they were speculating about why President Richards wanted to see them, neither of them wanted to actually say the word *bishop* out loud, even though it was in the back of both of their minds.

Sister Stephens spoke first, "Are you okay?"

"Yeah, I think so. Are you?" he asked.

She just sat there. Then the tears came.

"What's wrong?" he asked sincerely.

"I'm just a little worried," she admitted.

"About what?"

She took a deep breath and said, "I'm just concerned that the kids and I will never see you. My father was in the stake

---
4 In Conference Report, Apr. 1997, *Help, Bishop!*, Elder Dallin Oaks,

presidency when I was growing up, and he was always so busy with meetings and interviews that he missed everything.

"He was gone so much that a woman, who had recently moved into our ward, approached my mother at church one Sunday and invited her to go to a Single Adult activity." Sister Stephens choked out a little laugh through the tears as she thought back on that conversation.

She continued, "The woman was embarrassed for assuming that my mom was single, but who could blame her for jumping to that conclusion? My dad was so busy with his church responsibilities, that we rarely saw him—especially on Sundays. My mother raised her children mostly on her own."

Then, as Sister Stephens was wiping the tears away and trying to shake off the wave of unwanted emotion, she whispered a gentle request, "Being bishop is a more demanding job than stake president. Just promise me that we'll always be your *first priority*."

Brother Stephens reached over the center console, held his wife's hand, and smiled at her. He knew this was a big calling and that it would require huge sacrifices from his wife and kids, too. He didn't want this burden to affect his family, but he could see that it was already starting to.

He gave his wife's hand a little squeeze, looked her in the eyes and said, "I promise!" Then he said a silent prayer, right there in the car, and begged Heavenly Father to help him keep his word.

Chapter 3

The Stake President

"Simon, son of Jonas, lovest thou me? He saith unto him, Yea, Lord;
thou knowest that I love thee. He saith unto him, Feed my sheep."
John 21:16

"Now that you've had a few days to let everything sink in, do you have any concerns about the calling?" asked President Richards.

The stake president had asked Brother Stephens to come back to his office after prayerfully choosing counselors for the new bishopric. He could tell immediately that the newly called bishop was already struggling with something.

Brother Stephens took a deep breath and replied, "President, it's a little difficult to define. First of all, I've had a powerful feeling of love for the members of my ward."

He could see the stake president begin to smile and nod his head, so he took courage and pushed onward, "But there's also a deep sense of urgency and concern for the welfare of the people in the ward, even the non-members. It's almost a feeling of anxiety. I feel an enormous load, or burden pressing down on me. I don't know how to reconcile all those feelings..." he said as he trailed off, lost in his thoughts.

Regaining focus, he continued, "It's not as if I'm aware of any actual problems. All of the families in the ward are great. They are some of the best people I've ever met. But the Spirit keeps telling me that I'm not seeing the whole picture, and that there are a lot of needs in my ward. I get the impression that there's a lot of pain behind all the smiles. It's like the Lord is telling me that they need help, protection and love.

"So, to finally answer your question, I guess the thing that worries me most is that I may not be adequate for the job. I just don't know if I can do everything that needs to be done and still take care of the needs of my own family. I feel like the members of my ward need much more help than I can give them. I believe in inspiration President, but I'm worried that you may have chosen the wrong guy." Then he stopped talking and looked for direction and reassurance from his leader.

The smile on President Richards' face was bigger than ever, and Brother Stephens thought to himself, *Why is he still smiling? Didn't he hear a word I just said?*

President Richards chuckled for a moment, then slapped his hand down on the desk and said, "Brother Stephens, you're absolutely right! You can't do it all, and your ward does need a lot more help than you can give them!"

That definitely wasn't the response he expected. At first, he thought President Richards was just making fun of him, but the longer he sat there without saying anything, Brother Stephens knew he was missing the point of the president's declaration.

Then President Richards said, "Brother Stephens, I think I know you pretty well. I know that you're a great husband and father. I know you magnify the callings that you're given. I know you're self-employed, and that your business requires a lot of your time, and I know that you have many other obligations in your life right now."

President Richards paused for a second and then asked, "With all that you have going on, do you think you could do everything that is expected of you at home, as a husband and father, without the help of your sweet wife?"

Brother Stephens laughed out loud and answered with a resounding, "Not a chance! And my wife would tell you the same thing."

Without missing a beat, President Richards continued, "If you can't do everything you need to do at home without any help, then how can you possibly be capable of running an entire ward—that has more than 100 active families—without the help of others?"

Brother Stephens was starting to see where his leader was going with this.

President Richards continued, "You have been called as bishop, which is an enormous responsibility—one of the most demanding in the Church. You have been placed in charge of every person within your ward boundaries, member and non-member. Do you happen to know how many people that is?"

Brother Stephens looked confused and answered, "No. I've never actually counted."

The stake president smiled patiently and asked, "Do you think the Lord knows how many people He has assigned you to look after?"

He looked at his leader and nodded yes.

President Richards leaned forward in his chair again and said, "You see, the Savior has described the members of His church as a flock of sheep. He has also referred to himself as 'The Good Shepherd' and has told us that He loves His flock. He wants every single lamb to come home to Him. After His death and resurrection, the Savior returned and gave Peter and the other apostles the commandment: 'Feed my sheep.'

"Now, over two thousand years later, the Good Shepherd has given you a portion of His flock to guard and to feed."

The president continued, "This is a heavy responsibility, and it may seem overwhelming to you right now as you face the prospect of replacing your current bishop. But rest assured, the Lord has confidence in you, and He has provided a way for you to minister to the needs of every lamb in His flock and still take care of your own family."

> "He has provided a way for you to minister to the needs of every lamb in His flock, and still take care of your own family."

The stake president looked at Brother Stephens thoughtfully for a moment and moved the conversation in another direction, "You mentioned that you have already felt a deep love for the people in your ward. That tells me that you are already feeling the mantle of your calling, and you haven't even been set apart yet. You can feel it, can't you?"

Confused, Brother Stephens replied, "I don't know. I've always heard that a bishop can feel the mantle of his calling, but I could never fathom what that meant."

President Richards nodded and said, "What most people don't understand is that *every calling has its own mantle*. Primary teachers, deacons quorum presidents, and home and visiting teachers all have mantles associated with their callings, too. The mantle is really made up of two parts. One part is the *authority* associated with the calling, which might include keys, rights, privileges, powers, discernment, and the revelation that is necessary to magnify that calling.

"The second part of the mantle is *love*. That's what you're feeling now." The president paused to let that sink in.

He continued, "That feeling of love, which you began having immediately after the calling was extended, is a gift to you from the Savior. He loves each of His lambs individually. He knows we will protect the ones we love, so He shares a portion of His endless and unconditional love with those whom He has called as shepherds of wards, quorums, classes and families. The more you serve them, the more you will love them. That's the mantle. When you get released, it will pass to the next shepherd assigned to watch over and strengthen the sheep."

"That makes sense," said the new leader. "I couldn't understand why I felt connected so quickly. It was like the day I became a father. I couldn't imagine loving anyone as much as that new baby in my arms."

"Exactly. Just as a father loves his family, you will have an unconditional love for your ward members. Sometimes that love will be a source of great joy and happiness for you, and at other times it may seem overwhelming, agonizing and even bone crushing as those you are called to shepherd experience pain, suffering and heartache. As you give your time and energy to serve your new little flock, you will come to understand, as well as anyone on this earth, why the Savior would voluntarily suffer for our sins in the Garden of Gethsemane and sacrifice His life for us at Golgotha. It's because of the love He has for each of us.

"Now," exclaimed the stake president enthusiastically, "the first thing I want you to do is start reading the Handbook and prayerfully consider how you will implement what you learn.

"The second thing I want you to do is visit with Bishop Smith as soon as you have been set apart. He's the bishop of the Mountain Ridge Ward."

Puzzled, Brother Stephens asked, "Ok, but why Bishop Smith?"

"Because Bishop Smith has learned how to implement the Lord's method of shepherding His flock. It has made his calling so much easier. I wish more bishops would figure it out instead of trying to do everything themselves."

He continued with a sigh, "Unfortunately, most members of our church have a hard time doing things differently than what they've seen others do who have preceded them, including bishops. Most bishops become so busy addressing problems as they occur, they have little time to do much else. So when a new bishop gets called, he just naturally thinks that's the way the calling is done, and continues in the tradition of overloaded bishops by hoarding the troubles of the entire ward.

"Instead of running around putting out fires all of the time, the Lord wants us to extinguish the flames before they get out of control—or completely prevent them—*ideally without the bishops even getting involved.*"

President Richards looked at the new bishop, and with a little grin he asked rhetorically, "Brother Stephens, did you know that the bishop isn't the only person in a ward who can solve a problem?"

He continued, "And believe it or not, the Good Shepherd has given bishops a way to let others help carry the load. We just never realize the potential of the Lord's shepherding program, because most leaders have never seen it executed properly. Bishop Smith has figured it out and is shepherding the flock the way the Lord designed it to be done."

President Richards picked up his scriptures. He looked at them and then slowly said, "The Savior has given us modern-day revelation—through living prophets—to show us how to care for His flock. Ironically, it may be a paradigm shift for you and your ward, because we typically don't perform this assignment at the level the Lord would like to see it done. But once you help your ward learn their responsibility in the shepherding process, and use the program as it was designed to be used, you will see your ward come together like never before."

Then President Richards paused, looked straight at Brother Stephens, and then said, "But Bishop..."

Bishop. It still sounded odd to him, but he was starting to feel more comfortable with the idea of it.

The stake president continued, "...Bishop Stephens, when you are set apart, *you* will hold the keys for your portion of the Lord's flock. You will have many questions as you begin to serve in this calling, and He will have *all* of the answers that you are looking for. Be humble and prayerful, and through the Holy Ghost, the Lord will reveal *all things that you should do*. I promise you that."

After Brother Stephens left the stake president's office, he sat down in the foyer of the meetinghouse, took out a note pad from his briefcase, and wrote down some notes from his visit.

NOTES FROM STAKE PRESIDENT:

1. A bishop cannot satisfy all the needs of a ward and still take care of his first priority—his family. He needs help.

2. The bishop is not the only person in the ward who can solve a problem.

3. The Good Shepherd loves every member of His flock, and He has shared a portion of that love with his *under-shepherds* which helps motivate them to watch over and minister to the needs of the flock.

4. Implement the shepherding program as the Lord intended it to operate, based on your ward's needs and according to the revelation you receive for those you serve.

5. Trust and rely on the inspiration that is associated with the calling you hold. Be humble and prayerful, and the Holy Ghost will reveal *all things that you should do.*

Chapter 4

The Bishop

*"I don't know of any duty that is more sacred, or more necessary,
if it is carried out as it should be, than the duties of the teachers
who visit the homes of the people, who pray with them, who
admonish them to virtue and honor, to unity, to love, and to
faith in and fidelity to the cause of Zion."*[5]
President Joseph F. Smith

On the very day the new bishop was set apart for his calling, he promptly obeyed the counsel of the stake president and called Bishop Smith's executive secretary to set up an appointment.

When he arrived at the scheduled time, he was surprised that the veteran bishop was ready to see him. He had never met a bishop who wasn't always behind on interviews. They sat down, and Bishop Smith immediately gave Bishop Stephens both congratulations and condolences on his new assignment. After a few pleasantries, Bishop Smith smiled and kindly asked, "So what can I do for you?"

The new bishop responded, "President Richards told me that you have a new model for shepherding your ward that I am supposed to learn and follow. What's your secret?"

---

[5] In Conference Report, Apr. 1915, p. 140, President Joseph F. Smith

Bishop Smith smiled and replied, "Bishop, there is no secret. We simply follow the scriptures and the Handbook. The secret, if there is one, is to actually execute the program as the Savior intended."

He began to explain, "The Lord has given each of us authority over a small portion of His flock, even if it is just ourselves.

"First, we are to take personal responsibility for our own welfare, as best we can. I've heard it said that we should make sure we aren't on *The Lord's Worry List*. It's just like when you're on an airplane. In an emergency, you are counseled to secure your own oxygen mask first and then help the people closest to you. You can't help anyone else on the plane if you can't breathe for yourself. Likewise, before you can help anyone else come unto Christ, you need to gain your own testimony of the Savior and follow His teachings.

"After that, you are responsible for the spiritual and temporal welfare of your own immediate family.

"And finally, as it says in Section 20 of the Doctrine and Covenants, you are to 'watch over the Church always, and be with and strengthen them.'[6]

"In this ward, we try to follow these three steps of personal accountability and stewardship. It is really quite simple, and as our members have applied it, our ward has become a little City of Enoch."

---

[6] Doctrine & Covenants 20:53

19

This was awkward. Bishop Stephens had heard all of this before—self reliance and service for others. He thought that he was there to learn some new secret method of leadership from this more experienced bishop, and now he was being told there was no secret. He thought to himself, *Why would the stake president ask me to have this meeting?*

Then a little half-smile returned to the older bishop's face and he said, "You look confused Bishop. There is *one* thing we do that's a little different from the other wards in the stake. Do you want to know what that is?"

Bishop Stephens returned the smile and nodded eagerly. Anticipating a lengthy lecture on shepherding, he pulled out a pen and notepad so that he wouldn't forget a word.

Then the veteran leader leaned back in his chair again, and with a big smile he said, "In our ward, we do our home and visiting teaching as it was actually intended to be done."

"Huh?" whispered the new bishop, unaware that his question was even audible.

Bishop Smith repeated his counsel, "You heard me right. We home and visit teach."

Almost defensively, Bishop Stephens replied, "Well, we do that in our ward, too."

"Do you do it the way the Lord wants it done?" inquired Bishop Smith.

"I think so," said the new bishop. But after looking at Bishop Smith for a few more seconds, he admitted, "Actually, I don't know."

The bishop smiled again and said, "You're not alone. Most members—even bishops and stake presidents—can't answer that question, either. In fact, most people don't know what home teaching really is, or how much it can bless their lives."

> "Home and visiting teaching is the Lord's way of watching over his flock."

Then, in a very reverent tone, Bishop Smith quietly said, "The home and visiting teaching programs were divinely designed to accomplish two of the most vital purposes of the Lord. First, it is the Lord's way of watching over His flock and ministering to the needs of the lambs.

"Secondly—and I believe this is the most important reason the Lord created the program—our home and visiting teaching assignments are built-in *opportunities* for each member of the Church to develop the type of love that we are commanded to have for one another. A Christlike love. Charity."

Then he pointed to a frame on his wall that had the following quote, from President Ezra Taft Benson.[7] He read it out loud:

---

[7] In Conference Report, Apr. 1987, *To the Home Teachers of the Church,* President Ezra Taft Benson

"There is no greater Church calling than that of a home teacher. There is no greater Church service rendered to our Father in Heaven's children than the service rendered by a humble, dedicated, committed home teacher."

Bishop Stephens was silent. He looked at his empty notepad and wondered what to write. It couldn't be that simple.

Then he asked, "What is the home teaching percentage like in your ward?"

The bishop answered, "We don't care about percentages in this ward."

The new bishop thought to himself, *Only people that don't get good grades say that grades aren't important.* Then he asked, "Don't you keep records? How do you know if anyone is getting visited?"

"I didn't say that we don't keep records," said the bishop, "I simply said we don't care about the percentages. What I care about is how the families are doing and if their needs are being met. We have a very accurate reporting system, and we keep very detailed records. Probably the best in the stake."

Pressing for a number, Bishop Stephens inquired again, "Then what is the percentage you report?"

Reluctantly, the bishop replied, "Our home and visiting teachers consistently visit between 95% to 100% of the individuals in our ward—every month."

Bishop Stephens' jaw literally dropped open. He couldn't believe it. He had never seen a ward perform at such a high level before. He could not imagine how an entire ward consistently visited every home, month after month.

The veteran bishop continued, "I can see doubt in your eyes, but it's true. At least ninety-five percent of our families get an in-home visit, every month. Some of them are visited multiple times per month, depending on their situation.

"But once again, I want you to understand that I really don't care about the numbers, even when we visit 100% of the families. I only look at the statistics, because I know that the Savior cares about the welfare of 100% of His flock—not just 99% of it. There is no victory or bonus for bishops with good statistics. If there are families that are still in need of comfort, counsel, welfare, or love—and there always are—there is a need to continue to visit and minister in the homes. The actual visit is just the *minimum requirement* that the Lord has given us. It's hard to do any of the important things that He wants us to accomplish if we aren't, at the very least, visiting the home."

"Besides," Bishop Smith added, "statistics can only tell me where to look for problems that might be happening in the execution of the program. I need to know if there are any families with issues that actually require my attention. Statistics can't tell me if there are welfare needs, illnesses, conflicts in the home, overloaded families, underloaded families, testimony concerns, or anything else. But I can find those things out quickly through faithful and diligent home and visiting teachers reporting the status of their families to their leaders."

Then the veteran bishop shifted gears and said, "I have to be honest with you, though. I don't think that the titles *Home Teacher* and *Visiting Teacher* are entirely accurate. Teaching is an important part of our responsibilities as shepherds, but the true purpose of the program is to *minister* to the family's needs and concerns. I'm not terribly worried about a lesson actually getting taught every month, especially if the family has special needs. I sometimes wish we could call the program *Home Ministering.* That's a much more descriptive name, and a lot more consistent with how the scriptures describe a home or visiting teacher's responsibilities.

"Another thing that creates confusion—and sets the wrong expectation—is that we have connected reporting our visits to a *calendar month.* This gives people the incorrect impression that it's only a once-a-month obligation. The purpose of returning and reporting should be to pass along information about the welfare of the family, not simply announce that we made a visit. In my mind, *home ministering is never done.*"

Then he asked, "May I share a quote with you?"

Bishop Stephens loved what he was hearing and answered, "Yes!" with a little more enthusiasm than he would have liked.

Bishop Smith then pulled a piece of paper out of his desk. It was a little wrinkled, as if he had referred to it many times. Then he said very softly, "This is one of my favorite quotes, and it backs me up on what I just said about ministering. This is a quote from a talk given by James A. Cullimore during the October 1972 General Conference. It is one of the best talks given on the topic of home ministering. He was quoting President Harold B. Lee, and at the time this statement was originally made, home teaching had only been redefined for about a decade. President Lee was expressing his disappointment that the priesthood holders hadn't yet understood the true purpose of the program or caught the vision of what it could really do for the families in the Church."[8]

He then began reading very slowly to make sure Bishop Stephens heard every word:

> *"'Maybe the home teacher should be charged more clearly to describe his mission to watch over and to strengthen, to see that members do their duty. ...They think themselves as teachers of the Gospel message only. Maybe we ought to be calling them home guardians or sentinels and to report their stewardship to the fathers of the ward. We must do something to change the emphasis from teaching to guardians 'watching over the church' kind of concept. Until we get that into our minds, we are not going to do the kind of home teaching that is going to get results.'"*

---

[8] Quoted by Elder James A. Cullimore, in Conference Report, Oct. 1972, *Home Teachers—Watchmen Over the Church*

Bishop Stephens quipped, "It doesn't sound like we've progressed very much since that talk was given. He could have given that quote at the last General Conference."

"You're right!" responded Bishop Smith. "Keep in mind, however, even though he was talking about home teaching in that quote, you could easily insert the term visiting teaching as well. Visiting teaching is equally crucial in ministering to the needs of the ward. The difference between the two programs is that home teaching is a priesthood duty, not just an assignment. It is built directly into the priesthood responsibility of every man in the Church, from the office of Teacher to Apostle. In the same way that every worthy and able young man should serve a mission, every worthy and able priesthood holder should magnify his priesthood by home teaching.

"Visiting teaching, however, is an assignment within the Relief Society. The sisters are given more flexibility to minister to the women they're assigned to. Though a personal visit is best, the Handbook allows sisters to keep in touch in other ways, even a phone call or a note, especially when the assigned sister is not available. Nevertheless, it's important to understand that though the sisters' role in ministering to the flock is a little different from the men, it is equally important. In fact, in most cases, the sisters are a lot more open and honest about their needs and concerns with their visiting teachers than with the home teachers."

Bishop Smith continued, "There's another, more selfish reason I want the home and visiting teaching to be done the right way. *When it's being done properly, the bishop's job is much easier.* As you can see, nobody is knocking down my door to see me, but it wasn't always like this. The way I spend my time as bishop has changed dramatically since our focus changed to home ministering. Home teachers are now able to address a lot of their families' needs before they ever come to my attention.

"One example that comes to mind happened just last month. As is typical, my wife found out before I did that a family in our ward had an enormous crisis occur in their home. As soon as it was brought to my attention, I called the high priest group leader who had stewardship over this particular family. Not only was he already aware of the problem, but he reported that the home and visiting teachers had already visited with the family, addressed their needs and resolved the problem. He then apologized for not telling me as it was happening, but because the issue had been resolved so quickly, he decided that he would tell me at our next Ward Council meeting. He said he didn't want to bother me with a problem that was already resolved. I told him that if a problem has been resolved, then it's not a problem anymore, and I assured him that he did the right thing."

"When home teaching is being done properly, the bishop's job is much easier."

The bishop took a deep breath and concluded with conviction, "So, assuming that you have come here to learn how to magnify your calling, the single most important thing you can do as a leader is teach the members of your ward how to care for the families they've been assigned to minister to. Home and visiting teaching is the Lord's method of shepherding His flock and ministering to the needs of the ward members, and it's the way we develop love for one another within our wards."

"If that's the case, *how do your home teachers minister differently than everyone else?*" asked the new bishop.

"That is exactly the right question! For that answer, I'll direct you to a couple of other people. My secretary will give you their names and contact information."

Then Bishop Smith paused for a moment as if he were deciding whether or not to say something else. After a moment he said, "Bishop Stephens, you seem very sincere and open to receiving counsel and direction. If you would like, I'll share with you the best advice I ever received about being a bishop."

Bishop Stephens was still trying to process what he had already received, but he looked up at Bishop Smith and nodded.

"If you want to magnify your calling and still have time left over for your own family, which is your most important responsibility, then you need to delegate. Delegate everything you are allowed to delegate to your counselors, secretary, clerks, quorum leaders, and relief society. Delegate until you're embarrassed that you're delegating so much...and then delegate some more!"[9]

> *"Delegate until you're embarrassed that you're delegating so much...and then delegate some more."*

---

[9] Quote by Randall Gormley

Bishop Smith continued, "Bishop, that's what the *home ministering* program is. It is delegation—pure and simple. The Lord has delegated the work of shepherding His flock, which includes all the members of His Church. This is exactly what happened on the shores of Galilee when the resurrected Savior told Peter, 'Feed my sheep.'[10] The Lord was delegating the care of His flock to Peter, the new president of the Church, and the responsibility was so important that he repeated the charge three times in a row. The Good Shepherd was telling the under-shepherd: *If you love me, you'll feed my sheep.* We're under the same mandate in the Savior's restored Church.

"Today, our modern-day prophet, who holds all of the keys for the Church, delegates the shepherding to the stake president, who holds the keys for this geographical area of the flock. Then down to you and me, the bishops, who hold the keys for our wards. We then delegate the ministering duties to our quorum, group and Relief Society leaders. And finally, they delegate that responsibility to the home and visiting teachers.

"Keep in mind, delegation doesn't relieve me or you from our stewardship as bishops, but it allows us to share and spread the load so that we are not overwhelmed with the huge burden of ministering to well over 100 families. Not only would that be impossible, that's not what the Lord ever intended.

"Obviously, there are many issues we cannot delegate that are confidential in nature or specific to the calling of bishop, like

---

[10] John 21:16

the distribution of welfare resources, the duties of the president of the Aaronic Priesthood, overseeing the finances of the ward and being a judge in Israel. Of course, nobody in the ward besides the bishop, can take a confession and help someone through the repentance process. That's one of the things we must spend our time on.

"But, even though the bishop is the only one that can allocate the resources of the Bishop's Storehouse, that doesn't mean he's the only one that can help a person with a welfare issue. There are so many other people in the ward with talents, skills and the stewardship to assist their fellow members and help carry the load. The bishop can request help from others to assist in teaching a brother or sister how to write a resume, or how to interview for a job, or how to balance a budget. In fact, the home teachers can help coordinate all of that help."

Bishop Stephens jumped in and asked, "Losing a job and being on Church welfare is a pretty private matter, isn't it? Aren't people too embarrassed to let others know what's going on in their lives?"

"You're right. It *can* be embarrassing for some people. But it's the bishop's job to set the expectation early, especially in situations like these, that the goal is to get someone off Church welfare as soon as possible, and that we are going to use all of the resources that we have in our ward to help them, especially the men and women who were called by inspiration to directly minister to their needs. Most people understand and accept those conditions, and they appreciate the extra help.

"Home and visiting teachers are the true ministers in a ward and are vital to its spiritual health. And it's unfortunate that due to a lack of training, many of them don't fully understand just how important their responsibility is. In fact, for the men of the Church, only their duties as husband and father rank higher than their responsibility as home teacher. This is one of their most important priesthood duties. Almost all other callings in the ward or stake are support callings.

"You'll find that once you start shepherding the Lord's way, meaning that you stop looking at your home ministering responsibility as a 12-visit per year burden and start looking at it as a 365-day per year ministry, that's when you'll see the miracles begin to happen. Families will start having a change of heart and begin allowing their home and visiting teachers into their lives. They will start confiding in them, and more importantly, allowing them to help. It's only natural that when you feel loved unconditionally, you trust more easily and are much more willing to allow others to help. Eventually that love for one another will spread throughout the entire ward. The key is love—and when your are home ministering properly, love is a natural consequence."

"Home and visiting teachers are the true ministers in a ward."

Then Bishop Smith leaned forward in his chair and said, "But even with all the good that home ministering does in our ward for the families, I think I have finally figured out the most important spiritual benefit of the program—the real purpose for

32

its existence. I believe that *home and visiting teaching is really more for the home ministers than for the families being visited.* I believe that the callings of home and visiting teacher are really gifts—sacred gifts from our Father—to help us *become more like His Son.* As you begin to see how this program is supposed to work, you will understand how very true that is."

Bishop Stephens was in awe of the wisdom that was being shared. He felt the Spirit testify of the truth of this doctrine. He was excited to learn more, and he thanked his new mentor over and over for his time.

Bishop Smith stood, shook his protege's hand and said, "Come see me anytime. I love to help people that want to home and visit teach the Lord's way. It's so fun to see the results when they minister the way the Lord intended.

"But most importantly Bishop, if you're persistent and stick with the program as prescribed by the Lord, *and don't give up on it,* it will forever change the hearts and lives of the members of your ward."

NOTES FROM THE BISHOP:

1. "There is no greater Church calling than that of home teacher." - Ezra Taft Benson
2. Home and visiting teaching is the Lord's method of shepherding His flock.
3. Home and visiting teaching makes the bishop's job much easier.
4. Think of home and visiting teaching as *home ministering*.
5. Home ministers are vital to the spiritual health of a ward.
6. Home ministering is never done.
7. 100% home and visiting teaching is not the end goal, it's the *minimum* goal. You can't start to minister without first visiting the family.
8. Statistics are only able to tell you whether the family was visited, not what needs they have.
9. Bishops should delegate until they are embarrassed they are delegating so much, then delegate some more. It's the Lord's model.
10. Home and visiting teaching is a 365-day per year ministry.
11. Be persistent and don't give up on helping home and visiting teaching become home ministering.

Chapter 5

The High Priest Group Leader

"There can flow through this channel a redeeming spiritual power to the limits of heaven itself. Through home teaching, tragedies have been averted. Sinking souls have been lifted. Material need has been provided. Grief has been assuaged. The infirm have been healed through administration. While the work goes on without being heralded, it is inspired of Almighty God and is basic to the spiritual nourishment of this people."[11]
President Boyd K. Packer

The interview was over, and Bishop Stephens left the experienced bishop's office with many more questions than he arrived with. He looked at the list the executive secretary gave him, and the first name on the list was the high priest group leader, Brother Garner.

When he arrived, he was offered a seat and Brother Garner asked with a big smile and a booming voice, "So what do you want to know about home teaching?"

This time he was a little more prepared to answer that question. Bishop Stephens said, "Your bishop said that you do your home teaching differently than the other wards in the stake. I would like to know what you do?"

---

[11] In Conference Report, Oct. 1972, *The Saints Securely Dwell*, Boyd K. Packer

He replied, "We simply follow the Lord's model as it's spelled out in the scriptures. The scriptures teach us everything we need to know about home teaching."

He pulled out his scriptures and flipped through the pages until he found what he was looking for. Then he continued, "We are counseled in the 20th section of Doctrine and Covenants to do the following:

- Visit the home of each member.
- See that the Church meet together often.
- See that there is no hardness with each other.
- Exhort them to pray vocally and attend to all family duties.
- Warn, expound, exhort, teach and invite all to come unto Christ.

"And probably the most important thing we do as home teachers:

- Watch over the Church always and be with and strengthen them.[12]

"First and foremost, our home teachers visit the home of each member regularly—which means at least monthly, *more if needed.* They can't fulfill their calling without a visit.

---

[12] *Doctrine and Covenants* 20:53-59

"Second, they are called to watch over their families and identify what their needs are.

"Third, they do all that is within their power to minister to those needs as the Savior would.

"Fourth, the home teachers teach the Gospel principles in the homes and encourage their families to be obedient, kind, loving, forgiving and to come unto Christ.

"And of course, when the home teachers visit their families, they lovingly and respectfully ask how the families are doing with their prayers, scripture reading, Family Home Evenings, church callings, etc. They also ask if they need any help or encouragement fulfilling any of those duties. If a family isn't coming to church regularly, they invite them to attend and make them aware of any activities that are coming up. These are all basic things home teachers are commanded to do, but as the scripture states, they are mostly there to watch over the family, make sure their needs are being met, and support and strengthen them."

The new bishop interjected a question at this point, "Your home teachers actually ask if the family is praying and reading their scriptures?"

Brother Garner responded, "Yes, that's their job: To exhort the members to pray and attend to their family duties. But of course, as I said before, it needs to be done with love, respect and patience.

"Sometimes they might ask the father some of these questions privately, outside of the family visit, especially if they know that the family is struggling. Or if a family is not active at all, the home teachers will simply love them, fellowship them and invite them to return.

"However, every *active* family in our ward is already expecting those questions. The home teachers even ask each of the children how they are doing with their scripture reading, personal prayers or seminary. The more the home teachers inquire about those types of things, the more the family prepares itself to respond affirmatively the following month.

"Of course, as often as possible, we also teach the First Presidency message from the Church magazines, or some other customized lesson, if all the family's other needs are being met. The lesson always comes second to ministering to the needs of the family," said the veteran group leader.

"So lessons aren't that important in your ward?" asked the new bishop.

"Teaching and bearing testimony of Jesus Christ and His gospel are *very* important. We want to give a lesson and share our testimonies whenever possible, because we know when people hear gospel truths, the Holy Ghost will bear testimony to their hearts of those truths. In fact, Alma taught in the Book of Mormon, 'preaching of the word had a great tendency to lead people to do that which was just.'[13] But if a family is struggling with something specific, or requires some special attention, the home teachers are counseled to address those issues first.

---

[13] The Book of Mormon - Another Testament of Jesus Christ - Alma 31:5

"For example, if a family has an 11-year-old boy that is going to be receiving the priesthood in a couple months, a father may ask the home teachers to teach his son and family about the importance of the priesthood and the steps he can take to prepare for that event.

"If a child is getting baptized, or preparing for a mission, or struggling to gain a testimony, the head of the household may ask the home teachers to address those topics that better meet the needs of his family, rather than a message from the magazine that is less immediately applicable.

"But if a family is having a crisis in the home, sitting down together for 30 minutes to listen to home teachers give a lesson from a Church magazine may be more of a burden and distraction to them. That's when the home teachers need to adjust and serve in some other way to help the family. This is why it's so important that they use the Spirit in determining how to best address the family's most immediate needs.

"They may have the opportunity to give priesthood blessings, or relieve the pressure by helping with temporal duties like mowing the lawn or helping them get a car repaired. It may be that the most important thing they can do for a family one month is fast and pray for them. But they won't know what they can do without assessing the needs of the family on a regular basis, and as I have said, 'regular' may be much more often than just monthly.

"Does that make sense to you?" asked Brother Garner.

"Absolutely!" replied Bishop Stephens.

"To put it in its simplest terms, the answer to your question is this: If we home teach differently than the rest of the world, it's because *we look at ourselves as home ministers first, then home teachers second.*"

The young bishop was starting to understand. He nodded thoughtfully, reflecting on his own home teaching. Then he asked another question, "In our ward, some of the home teachers seem to have a problem getting together with their families. Don't you have that problem?"

The high priest nodded sympathetically and said, "The same thing still happens in our ward with a couple of families. There are always families that won't allow, or can't have the home teachers come over for a formal visit, but what matters is that the home teachers make an effort and let their families know that they are there for them, and that they are loved."

"What do you mean families '*won't allow* or *can't have*' the home teachers visit?" asked Bishop Stephens.

"Well, for instance, we have one less-active family that the home teachers visit every month, but so far, they have never been inside the home. The Handbook says we should set up appointments, but this family doesn't want an in-home visit. So the home teachers just started dropping by occasionally with goodies, or a little magnet quote for the refrigerator, or something for one of the kids on a birthday, but this is all done on the front porch.

> *"We look at ourselves as home ministers first, then home teachers second."*

"Each time they stop by, the smiles are warmer and the conversation lasts longer. They always inquire about the family's needs and if there is anything they can help with or *pray for during the month*. The family always declines, but they seem genuinely grateful for the offer. The home teachers may do that a couple of times a month, always trying to follow the Spirit and never pushing beyond what the family will let them do.

"We also have a few part-member families in our ward, as you probably have in yours. In one of the homes, the wife is a member, but the husband and children aren't...yet." Brother Garner smiled and winked as he added that last word.

"Most of the time the home teachers catch the husband on a good day, and he allows them to come visit his wife and kids. They always invite him to sit in the conversation, which he usually declines, but sometimes he'll sit near the room where the family is being taught and catch part of the lesson. He might even participate occasionally.

"But there are times that the husband won't let them visit at all, and we need to respect his wishes to help this sweet sister keep peace in the home. Some months, all that the home teachers can do is check in with the sister by phone and talk with her at church on Sundays, but they are in touch with her several times throughout the month. The most important thing to the bishop, and to the Lord, is that this family knows that their home teachers love them and that they are there for anything they need. The husband actually knows that now, too.

"One thing that has made a big impact on the husband is that *the home teachers always ask what the family needs them to pray for throughout the coming month.*"

That caught Bishop Stephens' attention. "The home teachers ask what they can pray for? You've mentioned that twice now. I like the sound of that! You say they do that every month?"

For a moment Brother Garner had almost forgotten that most people had never experienced home teaching the way his ward did it.

He then patiently explained, "Bishop, every home and visiting teacher in our ward has been asked to pray *daily* for each of their families—by name. This is one of the most important acts of service that the home ministers can do."

The new bishop was in awe. Why had he never heard this suggested before? Or had he? His mind was racing. To him, this single question, asked by a faithful home teacher, had so much potential to soften hearts and build trust.

Bishop Stephens looked at the high priest group leader with a childlike enthusiasm in his eyes. "That's fantastic! How long have you been doing this?"

"It actually started the first year our bishop was called. Every January he starts the new year with a simple challenge for everyone in the ward. One year his challenge was to research one of our own ancestors and complete the missing temple ordinances. Another time he challenged us to do one kind act for someone in our home every day that year. The purpose of these challenges is to create new habits in our lives.

"The first year he did this, he extended two challenges. The first challenge was to have all of the home and visiting teachers pray *each day* for the individuals they were assigned to teach. He challenged us to take a few extra minutes during our personal prayers and ask Heavenly Father to bless the people that we have a stewardship over as home ministers.

"The bishop reminded us that we have been commanded in the scriptures to *pray over our flocks daily,* and he invited us to remember the portion of the Lord's flock that each of us were assigned to 'watch over and strengthen.' He said that if we did this simple act of service, *our desire to visit and serve them would grow,* and as our service increased, so would our love for each of those families. Additionally, everyone in the ward would know that someone else was praying for their family, too.

"The second challenge was to have every home and visiting teaching companionship pray together before each visit.

"Now, I should probably add a disclaimer: These challenges aren't requirements in the Handbook. In fact, you might call them 'second-mile' or 'higher-law' challenges.

He continued, "I have to admit, at first, I implemented this challenge a little grudgingly. As I said, these were the first challenges he had extended to the ward, and a few of the ward members privately complained and murmured. They were a little put out that he would ask them to do anything more.

"Even I was a little bothered. Didn't I already have enough to pray about?" he asked sarcastically, and then winced, as if he were still embarrassed for ever thinking that.

43

"But then something amazing happened. One family that I was home teaching had several challenges, and I'll always remember the first time I asked Heavenly Father to bless them. As soon as I did, I literally heard Him tell me, 'Okay, I'll give you a hand, but we're going to help them together. This is what I want you to do for the family…,' and then the Holy Ghost began giving me a list of ways that I was going to help Father bless them.

"I was blown away! Heavenly Father was literally teaching me, right there on my knees, that He was going to use me to help this family. *I was going to be His ministering angel.*

"Sure, sometimes He intervenes with a miraculous healing, or jump-starts the weather for farmers in a drought, or parts a sea or moves a mountain, but usually our prayers are answered through the people around us. And who better to perform that service than the humble shepherds assigned to that family?

"I then started praying for the next family, and the next. Every time I poured out my heart for one of my families, thoughts came to my mind of things I could do to help each of them. Some were simple tasks, and some were more complex and time consuming. But in every case, my heart was beginning to change for each individual that I was assigned to watch over.

"It was a life changing experience for me and my companion. When we prayed together before visits, which we were already doing, our prayers were different. Then, when we would go into the homes, we quit asking the typical question,

'What can we do for you this month?' and began asking, '*What would you like us to pray for this month?*'"

The new bishop was mesmerized. He was lost in the story this good brother was telling. Everything he said made perfect sense and sounded so simple, yet it seemed so far away from his reach. *How do you get people to do this? How do you get people to care? How do you get people to trust and open up to their home teachers?* Then he said, "What an amazing story! What would people say when you asked them that question?"

"As you know, when you ask the family what you can do for them, they typically tell you that they are fine, and that they'll let you know if something comes up—but of course, they never do. When people are in need, they usually call a family member or a neighbor who they're more comfortable with to help them. If they need a priesthood blessing, they will wait until their problem has reached crisis-mode, and then they will call the quorum president or the bishop.

"From the very first month we started asking the families that question, the home teaching in our ward changed forever. At that very moment our conversations changed, our lessons changed, and our feelings for one another changed. Fathers began calling their home teachers to help with blessings, because they knew that the home teachers were sincerely concerned about each member of their family. Parents started speaking up and sharing private concerns about their children, or challenges at work, or spiritual questions that they had about the Gospel. Even the children would speak up and ask for the home teachers' prayers as they prepared for a big test or a sporting event.

"Everything changed. There began to be a level of trust between the families and the home teachers that I have never experienced before. It's a little slice of heaven here in our ward. We truly love our neighbors as ourselves."

Bishop Stephens could tell that this good brother had a testimony of home teaching and praying for his families. He decided to take advantage of a little pause the group leader took. The new bishop asked, "So how did you get everyone on board? Does every home teacher do this?"

Brother Garner responded, "Yes, most of them. At least they ask what they can pray for."

"How do you know?" asked the bishop.

"Well first of all, there is an expectation now by the families that their home teachers will ask that question, especially since the bishop issued The Challenge to the entire ward. There's nothing like having the bishop set a specific expectation from the pulpit!" He once again smiled and winked. *This guy is a winker*, thought the bishop as they laughed about that together.

"Also, we are getting reports back that the kids are now starting to remind home teachers if they forget to ask *The Question*. The children want to make sure the home teachers are praying for their special needs each night, too. Thank goodness for the kids!" Again, the two men laughed.

"And finally, we ask the home teachers in our monthly Home Teaching Interviews if there is anything we as a group leadership can be helping with or praying for."

With that, the Bishop perked up again. He quickly asked, "Home Teaching Interviews? You do those every month? The Handbook only says they are to be done 'regularly.'"

The group leader looked directly at the bishop and asked rhetorically, "What does 'regularly' mean? Couldn't it mean monthly, or even weekly? Every ward is different. Our ward chose to keep closer tabs on the families, so we decided to have the interviews on a monthly basis."

Bishop Stephens responded with a little chuckle, "I've had a couple of Personal Priesthood Interviews over the years, but I can't remember ever having a Home Teaching Interview. What do you do in those interviews each month?"

Brother Garner looked at his watch and said, "Bishop, that is another very important conversation that I don't have time for right now. I actually have a home teaching obligation. One of the young women in a family I home teach has a track meet over at the high school in about 20 minutes, and she invited me to come cheer her on. I hope you understand, but she is expecting me, and I don't want to let her down.

"Besides, the one you should talk to about Home Teaching Interviews is Brother Baugh, the elders quorum president. He's perfected them."

NOTES FROM HIGH PRIEST GROUP LEADER:

1. Use Section 20 of Doctrine and Covenants and *Handbook 2 - Administering the Church* as your model and instructions for home teaching.
2. Home teachers should lovingly and patiently inquire if their families are having regular family prayers and attending to their duties.
3. Home teachers should warn, expound, exhort, teach and invite all to come unto Christ.
4. Ministering to the needs of your family is the first priority; teaching a lesson is the second priority.
5. Lesson topics should be based on the needs of the family, not always the monthly Church magazine theme.
6. Home teachers should regularly ask their assigned families what they can be praying for.
7. Home teachers should pray *every day* for their families by name.
8. Home teachers should pray together as a companionship before each home teaching visit.

Chapter 6

The Elders Quorum President

"Brethren, home teaching is not just another program. It is the priesthood way of watching over the Saints and accomplishing the mission of the Church. Home teaching is not just an assignment. It is a sacred calling...a program that touches hearts, that changes lives, and that saves souls; a program that has the stamp of approval of our Father in Heaven; a program so vital that, if faithfully followed, it will help to spiritually renew the Church and exalt its individual members and families."[14]
President Ezra Taft Benson

When Bishop Stephens sat down with the elders quorum president he was immediately impressed. President Baugh was in his mid 20's, newly married and very confident in what he was doing as the president of his quorum.

After the initial get-to-know-you conversation, the new bishop said, "Brother Garner informed me that you are the *Fountain of Truth, Knowledge and Wisdom* when it comes to Home Teaching Interviews. Will you tell me how those interviews help you in this ward?"

President Baugh knew Bishop Stephens was just trying to butter him up, but he blushed a little nonetheless. He could also

---

14 In Conference Report, Apr. 1987, *To the Home Teachers of the Church,* President Ezra Taft Benson

tell the new bishop had been on quite a journey of discovery, as he once had when he first moved into the ward.

"Well Bishop, this has been a great learning experience for me, too. I have come to love our bishop, this ward and especially my quorum brothers. It is an honor to be their temporary leader, and I thank Heavenly Father every day for the privilege of being associated with these men. We have all grown a lot since our bishop's challenge. This single principle has taught us all that we can truly change lives by magnifying our priesthood as home teachers."

The bishop jumped in and asked, "Your bishop tells me that nearly every family gets visited at least monthly, sometimes more. That just amazes me! How do you get everyone to do their home teaching every month? How is that even possible? Do you do it for the ones that don't home teach?"

"That's a great question," responded the president. He continued, "And the answer to the second part of it is—No. We don't fill in the numbers by home teaching in place of a quorum member that misses a family. That would defeat the purpose of the record keeping. That doesn't mean that the presidency doesn't go visit and check in on families that we have concerns about, especially those that get missed, but we don't count our contact with the family as a home teaching visit.

"The bishop always reminds us that the numbers tell him nothing about the welfare of the families. The reason we keep statistics accurately, without padding or exaggerating them, is to let the bishop know which families are really being seen by their home teachers, and which ones are not. That's all you can really glean from a missed family on a statistical report, and those are the first families he asks about in our Priesthood Executive Committee or Ward Council meetings.

"And just because a family was visited, it doesn't guarantee all is well in the home. A family that is visited 100% of the year could be one of the families with the most difficult needs in the ward, and usually is. On the other hand, a family that gets missed every month may be one of the strongest families in the ward. If all that we report to the bishop is a number, then what can he know about the condition of each lamb in his flock? That's why we are doing the Home Teaching Interviews.

"When I was called to this position, the bishop had just extended what we now call 'The Challenge' to the ward. He told me that the most important duty I have as president is to oversee the home teaching in the quorum and to teach the quorum members how to minister the way the Lord would. He added that teaching them how to properly 'return and report' on the welfare of each family was an essential part of their responsibility. He made it perfectly clear that he didn't ever want us to report that the home teaching was 'all done.' He is famous for saying, '*Home ministering is never done.*'"

"I like that!" exclaimed Bishop Stephens.

President Baugh was nodding in agreement, then he said, "The home teachers should be reporting on the welfare of each

"Home ministering is never done."

51

family, even down to the individual, especially if there are issues. In fact, after ministering to the needs of the family, the second most important responsibility of the home teacher is passing on a report of the family's status to the bishop.

"He also reminded me that *returning and reporting is an eternal principle*. Even the Savior was required to return and report His stewardship to Father in Heaven. Our bishop once asked me, 'If the Creator of the universe was required to return and report, shouldn't we follow that example?'"

Bishop Stephens was impressed, but he couldn't understand how the presidency could possibly interview each companionship every month. He then asked, "Do you call each companionship on the phone every month for a report?"

The president smiled. "No. They are expected to call us. But it didn't start out that way. We used to meet personally with each companionship every month."

The surprise in Bishop Stephens' expression was obvious.

President Baugh continued, "Initially, when The Challenge was first given, the home teaching in our ward was pretty inconsistent, so the bishop asked me to start having monthly sit-down interviews with a member of each companionship to get a full report on their assigned families."

Bishop Stephens finally interrupted, "That sounds incredibly time consuming. Wasn't it hard holding that many interviews?"

"It wasn't hard at all. I'm sure that you, as a bishop, have a lot more meetings every month than we do," he said with a smile.

Bishop Stephens acknowledged that fact with a reluctant nod.

President Baugh continued, "As for the interviews, we only have about 60 elders in the ward, so that meant 30 interviews. After dividing them between me and my counselors, that was only 10 monthly interviews for each of us. We could easily meet with 2-3 elders each week, and we still had time for the in-home family visits that we do as a presidency, and the annual Personal Priesthood Interviews. It kept our secretary busy, but he needed the extra blessings anyway, so he was fine."

The new bishop laughed at that one. Then he asked, "Have you ever considered calling Home Teaching Coordinators?"

President Baugh answered, "That's not actually an official calling in the Church. Besides, the Handbook suggests that the home teachers report back directly to the elders quorum presidency or the high priest group leadership. This makes sense especially when you are dealing with feedback that is personal in nature. All *confidential* or sensitive information should be reported directly to the president or group leader."

When he could see that the bishop was satisfied with that answer, President Baugh pressed on, "The first month we did the interviews we met with both members of the companionship, together. We explained the purpose of a Home Teaching Interview, and the difference between a home teacher and a home minister. We also explained that we were looking for a report on the welfare of the family each month, instead of just telling us they had finished their home teaching. We started out this way, because our bishop believes that setting proper expectations is crucial when extending any new calling or assignment. After that initial interview, we began alternating between companions every other month.

"It's not required, but we like to start each Home Teaching Interview with a kneeling prayer when possible, which we ask the home teachers to offer. The home teacher then gives an accounting for each lamb in his flock, and they let us know if there are any individuals that have special needs. They tell us what they are doing to help the families and if they need our help or our prayers. If they need more help than the two companions can handle by themselves, they've been asked to come to the interview with a plan of action. We take note of what we as a presidency can do to help, and that becomes an agenda topic at our next presidency meeting.

"If a family requires immediate action, we drop everything and help the home teachers with whatever they need, or we rally the quorum troops if necessary.

"If a situation demands the bishop's help, which is very rare, we don't hesitate to call and let him know immediately. The bishop wants a list of all our concerns as they occur, not just at the end of the month. If a family is in need, or a youth is in danger, or if the home teachers need the bishop's help in any way, he wants to know as soon as possible. If all is well, we give him our report at the next Priesthood Executive Committee or Ward Council meeting.

"But once again, if there is an emergency, the home teachers know that they can call any of us immediately, 24-hours a day, instead of waiting for the interview."

The mechanics of the program were fascinating to Bishop Stephens. He was nodding and taking notes as fast as he could write.

President Baugh continued, "At the end of the interview, we always express our love for the home teacher and his companion, and then the presidency member offers the closing prayer.

"The home teachers that were already consistently visiting their families were able to report on their status without a problem, and those interviews only lasted about ten to fifteen minutes."

The bishop shrugged his shoulders and said, "That sounds like it's simple enough, and very effective. I'm still amazed that your whole ward bought into the program so fast."

The elders quorum president sighed and then said, "It wasn't exactly *simple*. There were some home teachers that were having problems making their visits before The Challenge and struggled initially after we started with the interviews. At first, some of them wouldn't even come to the interview.

"The ones that weren't home teaching before the changes were a little nervous, because they didn't know their assigned families well enough to report on their welfare. In those cases, we were the ones telling them how their families were doing in the interview.

"We challenged the companionship to make a visit that week and return and report. There were a lot of excuses at first. Some of them blamed their assigned families or their companions for their inability to home teach. In those cases, we simply asked them if they needed our help as a presidency in setting up the appointment or home teaching with them. Of course, they all declined, as they realized they were just as capable of accomplishing their assignment as the presidency was.

"Amazingly, almost every one of the home teachers who had previously failed to contact and teach their families were able to make a visit, and as requested, they returned and reported on their status."

"Really? That's an incredible turnaround!" exclaimed Bishop Stephens. He was genuinely impressed.

President Baugh nodded in agreement, "Some of our quorum members had never really understood *why* home teaching was so important and what its true purpose was, partly due to lack of training or even a lack of emphasis from previous ward leaders.

"Unfortunately, in most wards, there isn't a formal home teaching training program for the youth when they are teachers or priests in the Aaronic Priesthood. If your first home teaching experience is with a companion that doesn't have a testimony of the program—just like in the mission field—you will have a hard time breaking the cycle of mediocre ministering," he said shrugging, as if reluctantly accepting the reality of the situation.

"Once we implemented these interviews with our quorum members, and testified that home teaching was the Lord's method of shepherding His flock and ministering to each family's needs, they began to realize that it wasn't merely a suggestion, but actually a requirement of a priesthood holder in-good-standing. That's when they started making a real effort, and it became a top priority for each of them. Like most people, they just didn't understand the *true purpose* of home teaching. Once they understood, their actions changed."

Bishop Stephens then asked, "Were there any that resisted the change, and what did you do to get them onboard?"

The elders quorum president nodded and then explained, "If a companionship missed a family two months in a row, we would call both companions back in for the next Home Teaching Interview. We would again ask if they needed our help in fulfilling their assignment. This time, every companionship committed to complete their assignment the following month.

"After the first two months, only one priesthood holder in the entire ward hadn't come in to report his stewardship."

"What do you do in that type of situation?" asked the new bishop.

President Baugh smiled and said, "If a Melchizedek Priesthood holder doesn't home teach three months in a row—for a full quarter—Bishop Smith does the Home Teaching Interview. So that home teacher got a call from the bishop."

Bishop Stephens' interest had now piqued, "So what happened?"

The president smiled and responded, "When the home teacher went into the bishop's office, he didn't know what the interview was for. The brother was invited to open the interview with a prayer, just as we do in our Home Teaching Interviews. Bishop Smith then expressed his love for the brother and thanked him for his service in his ward calling. Then he asked just one question: 'Brother Jones, is your calling in the ward overloading you too much?' The brother was surprised and responded, 'No. Why?' The bishop then reminded him about The Challenge and told him that aside from his responsibility as husband and father, no other calling in the Church was as important to the Savior as the assignment of home teacher.

"Bishop Smith explained to this good brother that he was assigned as a home teacher, not called or set apart, because the responsibility had been built right into his priesthood—it came with the ordination. He also reminded him of the Oath and Covenant of the Priesthood as found in Section 84 of the Doctrine and Covenants. He told him that magnifying his home teaching assignment was one of the responsibilities that was required of him to keep his promise to Heavenly Father to magnify his priesthood.

"Bishop Smith lovingly explained how important his assigned families were to the Lord. He told the brother that he had been assigned by inspiration to minister to those families, and that the commandment given to priesthood holders to home teach was far more important to the bishop, and to

Heavenly Father, than his Sunday School calling was, especially because he had made a covenant to do it.

"After Bishop Smith bore his testimony to the home teacher, he read him the parable of the hireling."

"Ouch! That was a little harsh, wasn't it?" asked Bishop Stephens.

The faithful elders quorum president promptly defended his bishop by saying, "Not at all. Even the Savior gently rebuked His apostles when they weren't living up to His expectations. The bishop represents the Savior and is appointed to protect and feed the flock.

"Are you familiar with the parable of the hireling?" asked President Baugh.

Bishop Stephens knew the parable very well, but asked the president to share his thoughts about it anyway.

President Baugh opened his scriptures to John and read the following:

> "*I am the good shepherd: the good shepherd giveth his life for the sheep.*
>
> *But he that is an hireling, and not the shepherd, whose own the sheep are not, seeth the wolf coming, and leaveth the sheep, and fleeth: and the wolf catcheth them, and scattereth the sheep.*
>
> *The hireling fleeth, because he is an hireling, and careth not for the sheep.*

'I am the good shepherd, and know my sheep, and am known of mine.

'As the Father knoweth me, even so know I the Father: and I lay down my life for the sheep.'"15

The elders quorum president then said, "Now compare 'the hireling' to the story in the Book of Mormon about Ammon, protecting King Lamoni's flocks at the peril of his own life.16 He fought off multiple attackers with a sword to guard the king's sheep while others ran away and hid." He paused for a few seconds to let Bishop Stephens think about the contrast of those two stories as they related to home teaching.

The young man continued, "There are some people in the Church who feel we should let a person fail in a calling for the *learning experience* and suggest that we are taking away a person's agency if we don't. I disagree, especially with home teaching. First of all, the responsibilities of a home teacher are too important to allow for failure as part of some big test. Too many individuals can be affected by inattentive home teachers.

"Secondly, Heavenly Father employs consequences all the time for those that don't keep their *covenants*. If a priesthood holder flat-out refuses to pay tithing, obey the Word of Wisdom or attend his priesthood meetings, he may lose temple privileges.

---

15 John 10:11-15

16 The Book of Mormon - Another Testament of Jesus Christ - Alma 17:25-39

"We forget sometimes that there are requirements and responsibilities that come with bearing the priesthood of God. It isn't something we have a right to possess. We earn and retain the privilege through righteous behavior and good works.

"President Ezra Taft Benson said, 'There is no greater calling in the Church than that of home teacher.' The Lord desires *Ammon-like shepherds* that will protect His flock with their own lives, or in other words, with their time, talents and spiritual gifts. We definitely do not need more hirelings.

"This is one of the most dangerous times in the history of the world. The sheep are in great danger. There are many different types of wolves out there in the world. We must have vigilant shepherds to guard and feed the sheep."

> *"The Lord desires Ammon-like shepherds that will protect His flock."*

President Baugh opened up his scriptures again and said with a little smile, "My father would read this scripture to the boys who dated my sisters when we were growing up…just to scare them a little. But I think it applies to home teaching, too:

"*'For what shepherd is there among you having many sheep doth not watch over them, that the wolves enter not and devour his flock? And behold, if a wolf enter his flock doth he not drive him out? Yea, and at the last, if he can, he will destroy him.'*"[17]

---

[17] The Book of Mormon - Another Testament of Jesus Christ - Alma 5:59

Bishop Stephens laughed out loud. "I like the way your dad operates! I have to admit though, I love how that verse describes a protective, watchful home teacher."

Then he asked, "So what happened to the home teacher that was called into the bishop's office?"

"Well, it turned into quite the success story," the quorum president said. "Prior to the interview with the bishop, this man hadn't home taught in years. He had actually *refused* to go. He also didn't like having the home teachers come over to his house, probably because his home teachers had been doing it all wrong and were just wasting his time.

"After the bishop shared the story about the hireling, he told Brother Jones that he loved him and that he would do anything to help him magnify his responsibility as a home minister, even release him from his other callings if the load was too much.

"The bishop described some of the issues that his assigned home teaching families were dealing with, which Brother Jones admitted he was unaware of. Bishop Smith asked him to commit to return and report directly back to him when he had visited with the families, identified their needs and had a plan of action to help them. Brother Jones committed to visit his families and return and report on their status and on his plan of action. Then the bishop concluded the interview as we do, with a prayer, once again expressing his love for the brother.

"This good brother is now one of the most faithful home ministers in our ward. He is a 100% home teacher every month, and there is not a person he home teaches who doesn't love and appreciate him. The Lord has since trusted him with some of the most demanding callings in the ward."

The great quorum president continued with conviction, "Our bishop loves every member of our ward. We all feel that love. He recognizes how important home teaching is to nourishing each lamb in his flock. That's why the bishop has asked us to perform this responsibility at a higher level, and that's why he is even willing to release us from our other callings —whatever they might be—if we are having difficulty honoring our covenant to magnify our priesthood."

The elder then seemed to realize that the mood had shifted to a very serious one, so he quickly tried to change the tone saying, "It's important to understand that what we do in our ward is not a Church-wide requirement. The Handbook doesn't require a monthly interview. It only calls for home teachers to report on their families monthly. Meeting with them in person is what our bishop asked us to do to jump-start the program, but in some remote areas in the world, that's physically impossible. It's up to each Ward Council to determine, by revelation, what will work best to motivate their members to *home minister* at a higher level and keep improving over time.

"It's also vital that you realize that these interviews are done in a loving, caring way. Our home teachers feel our love and appreciation for them, and for the families that they teach. They hear us pray for them and express our love for them. We sincerely offer our full support and help if they are struggling to fulfill an assignment. And if a teaching assignment or companionship change needs to be made, for whatever reason, we address those needs in the interview.

"Now that we have set the expectation for what the Lord wants from a home teacher, the home teachers call us with their monthly reports, instead of face-to-face interviews. The phone interviews are exactly the same, just without the prayer. With the valiant home teachers, we only do quarterly sit-down interviews.

"If a companionship misses one of their families a couple times, my secretary calls them and sets up a personal interview. It only takes one *refresher interview* and they are back on track."

Bishop Stephens was learning so much from this young man. He had no doubt of the president's love for his quorum and had to assume that every member of his quorum felt it, too.

President Baugh looked at the bishop in front of him and asked, "Have you spoken to President Mann yet?"

"No. Who's that?" the bishop asked.

President Baugh looked a little surprised and said, "He's our Teachers Quorum president. Isn't he on also your list?"

Bishop Stephens looked at his list again. Sure enough, there was Harrison Mann. The bishop actually knew this young man by his nickname Harry, who was a good friend of his own 15-year-old son.

President Baugh then said, "Oh, you have to talk to him. He's making a huge difference in the home teaching program in this ward!"

"He is? How's a 15-year-old doing that?" he asked incredulously.

"Go ask him yourself. He loves to talk about home teaching," laughed President Baugh.

The bishop couldn't wait to hear more. This journey was proving to be one of the most eye-opening learning experiences that he ever had with regard to his own priesthood responsibility and how the Church should function. But learning from a young man the age of his own son? He couldn't track Harry down fast enough.

NOTES FROM ELDERS QUORUM PRESIDENT:

1. Returning and reporting our stewardship is an eternal principle.
2. Quorum presidencies and group leaderships should hold 10-15 minute Home Teaching Interviews monthly.
3. Interviews are done with love and patience.
4. The primary purpose is to ascertain the spiritual health and temporal welfare of each family.
5. Secondary purpose is to express appreciation and love for home teachers and offer help if needed.
6. Beginning and ending each interview with a prayer invites the Spirit to help direct the discussion.
7. Report all immediate needs to the bishop.
8. Don't be afraid to lovingly hold priesthood holders accountable for their stewardship.
9. The priesthood leaders in the ward need to gain testimonies of the Lord's way of shepherding and be on-board with home teaching interviews.
10. Help home teachers understand their role as teacher, minister, guardian and shepherd.
11. Note: Holding face-to-face monthly interviews is not a requirement in the Handbook, but they are effective in helping jump start this program and emphasizing the need to report on the welfare of the families.

Chapter 7
The Teachers Quorum President

"The teacher's duty is to watch over the church always, and be with and strengthen them; And see that there is no iniquity in the church, neither hardness with each other, neither lying, backbiting, nor evil speaking; And see that the church meet together often, and also see that all the members do their duty."
Doctrine and Covenants 20: 53-55

Harrison Mann was your typical 15-year-old boy. He was starting to notice that girls were not horrible, he loved the new music as loud as he could stand it, and the clothes he wore were even louder. But he was also unlike most 15-year-olds in the real world. He was an Eagle Scout, as were many of his closest friends. He was the first to raise his hand when volunteers were needed, and he was the last to leave the service project to go home. He was respectful to his teachers at school and at church, and polite to all the young ladies. He obeyed and loved his parents and wasn't embarrassed to hug them in public. He was concerned for his sisters and looked out for them at school. This was a really good kid.

When Bishop Stephens set up this meeting with Harry, the boy told the new bishop he was glad to meet and answer any of his questions, but would only have about 30 minutes. He had told Bishop Stephens that he needed to go home teaching and didn't have much time.

When he arrived, Bishop Stephens jumped right in with the questions to keep the boy on schedule. "So, Harry...," said the bishop, "...I'm told you're a great quorum president. President Baugh is very impressed with you and said that I needed to talk to you to get a better understanding of home teaching in your ward. Can you tell me what you're doing?"

The young man smiled at the compliment and replied, "We're having a lot of fun as a quorum doing our home teaching. We get along really well as a group, and we are trying to make a difference in the ward. It's been really fun!"

Fun? He had never heard a young man call church service "fun" before—especially home teaching. The bishop's interest continued to grow as he asked his next question, "I've been talking to your bishop and the other quorum leaders in your ward and they are doing things that I've never seen before. How do you fit into that puzzle and what do you do differently from the other teachers quorums in the stake?"

> *"Home teaching is our most important duty to God besides taking care of our own families"*

Harry smiled and responded, "When I was called to serve as the quorum president, our bishop told me that I was in charge of training the quorum to be good home teachers. He always says that home teaching is our 'primary duty to God.'"

"Your duty to God? I like that! It really is your duty to God, isn't it?" asked the bishop.

"Yep! Bishop Smith told me that home teaching is our most important duty besides taking care of our own families," he responded.

"Harry, why did your bishop put you in charge of the home teaching training and not your quorum advisors or the Young Mens president?" asked the bishop sincerely.

The young man looked at his friend's father a little bewildered and said very respectfully, assuming the bishop should have already known the answer to that question, "My bishop told me I am responsible for training my quorum, *because I hold the keys.*"

Bishop Stephens leaned back and smiled. He knew that he liked this kid, and now he was beginning to appreciate him on a whole new level. He realized very quickly that this was a mature young man and that he took his calling very seriously.

The bishop confirmed, "That's absolutely right, you do have that authority." Then he paused, thought about that for a second, and asked another question with much more respect in his voice, and this time he addressed this young leader appropriately, "President Mann, what do you do to train your quorum members?"

President Mann answered, "Well, one of the things we do every week in priesthood meeting, before our lesson, is have a *Home Teaching Moment.* That's where we invite a quorum member to talk about a neat experience he had home teaching that month, and how that experience was an opportunity to *magnify his priesthood.* Sometimes a member of the presidency will talk about a home teaching technique."

"Impressive! Did your bishop ask you to do that?" asked Bishop Stephens.

The young man replied, "No. When we were called, he told us to pray about how we could help the other boys in our quorum develop stronger testimonies of home teaching, and we all felt this was one of the things we should do."

"Really?" asked the bishop. "Give me an example of a Home Teaching Moment."

President Mann explained, "Well, last week it was my turn, and I shared an experience I had earlier that week. My father and I home teach an elderly couple, and the lady has been really sick. One night, my dad got a call right as I was getting ready to go to bed. About ten minutes later, he came into my room all dressed up in his suit and told me that Brother Johnson had asked him to give Sister Johnson a blessing. My dad normally takes me with him when he gives a blessing to one of our home teaching families, even though I can't help him in the circle. He says that he wants me to see how blessings work as often as I can, so when I become an elder and serve a mission, I will be prepared to give blessings, too."

The bishop was smiling and listening very intently. The young man continued, "But this time was different. My dad said that Brother Johnson asked him to come alone, because Sister Johnson was in bed and couldn't get downstairs. Brother

Johnson told my dad to let me know that he loved me and hoped I would understand. I could tell she was really sick.

"My dad told me the way I could help him this time, as his companion and her home teacher, was to pray that he would be able to give the blessing she needed, and to pray for Sister Johnson to get better quickly. So that's what I did, and she started feeling better the very next day.

"In my Home Teaching Moment, I bore my testimony to the quorum about how important it is to pray for our families to be well, and also to pray for ourselves and our companions to be inspired.

"In Home Teaching Moments we also learn about ways we can improve as home teachers by asking how our families are doing with their personal and family prayers or their Family Home Evenings, or we discuss new ways we can serve them. We also talk about how important it is to be praying for each family member daily. Stuff like that."

"So are you praying every day for each of the families you home teach, too?" Bishop Stephens asked.

"Yep, every day," said the young president.

Bishop Stephens had started taking notes again. He had never seen a teachers quorum focus on home teaching as their "primary" duty to God.

"Anything else?" he asked, knowing that the boy was on a schedule.

"We also use the Home Teaching Moment to announce what types of service that the families we home teach need each week, and we coordinate help from the quorum to get that done as soon as we can. Once a month, we do service for one of our weekly Mutual activities, and the Home Teaching Moment is the perfect way to find things to do. Sometimes we also have to do a service project on a weekend morning, because there are so many families in need."

"That's another great idea! But if your ward is like ours, you only have the same two or three boys show up for service projects that end up doing all the work, right?" asked the bishop.

"No, most of them show up. Sometimes, one of the guys will have a soccer game or a family activity or something, but almost everyone comes for service projects, and it never takes very long. *The work goes so much faster when we do it as a quorum.* Besides, we always have a lot of fun and the families usually feed us treats! We love doing service," said Harrison.

"That's so great. I'll bet the families you home teach really appreciate it, don't they?" asked the bishop.

"Yeah, they really do," the boy agreed. "One time, a lady we were helping said she felt like she had ten home teachers. That's the other really cool thing that has happened. All of us have gotten to know each others' home teaching families really well. It hasn't just made us really close as a quorum, we have also become really close as a ward."

That couldn't have been explained better by an experienced and seasoned high priest, thought the new bishop.

"Is there anything else you can tell me about Home Teaching Moments, President Mann?" asked Bishop Stephens.

"Not really," he said. "The only other thing we do is remind the boys about their Home Teaching Interviews. Do you know what those are?"

The bishop chuckled, and said, "Thanks to your ward, I know what they are now! We don't do those in our ward yet, but we will very soon!" Then the bishop asked, "But President Baugh didn't tell me that he also interviews the boys."

President Mann responded, "He doesn't. My counselors and I do the interviews for our quorum."

The bishop looked at Harry with a surprised look on his face, but he didn't know what to say.

Harry responded, "Bishop Smith said that we need to do them because we have a responsibility to follow up on our quorum members' stewardship, too. The elders quorum president and high priest group leader are in charge of the home teaching programs, but the bishop asked us to hold a ten minute interview with each member of our quorum also, and make sure that they're magnifying their callings as home teachers. We divide up the quorum between the three of us, and we each do about two or three interviews every month. My secretary switches it up every month so we each get to see everyone in the quorum on a regular basis.

"We start the interview by kneeling together in prayer. We always ask the quorum member to say the opening prayer. We ask them about their families, find out if there are any new service opportunities, and we ask if there are any needs that we need to report to the bishop. Usually those types of things are reported to the bishop through the other quorum leaders, but every once in a while, one of our quorum members will report something that wasn't reported by his adult companion. But the bishop doesn't want anything that is confidential to be discussed in Home Teaching Moments during class. Our quorum members understand that confidential things need to stay private, and they are only discussed in these interviews."

President Mann took one more deep breath and then said, "We also share a quick spiritual thought and bear our testimony. We always make sure we thank the boy for his service. Then a member of the presidency offers the closing prayer."

This young man was being trained by a wise bishop to become a great leader. He couldn't believe how much he had been entrusted to do. Of course he should be interviewing his quorum and checking on their stewardship. He held the keys to do that. No wonder this quorum was so tight knit. No wonder they all showed up to serve each other's families. No wonder this ward was so close. It was brilliant!

He wanted to keep asking questions but knew the young man was on a tight schedule. Then Bishop Stephens said, "I appreciate all the time you have spent with me. I wish I could take more of your time, but I don't want to make you and your father late for your home teaching appointment."

As if not even thinking about the mistake, Harry casually replied, "Oh, I'm not going with my dad. My first counselor is my home teaching companion for the boy that we teach."

That caught Bishop Stephens off guard. "What? Your companion is another boy from your quorum? Don't you need an adult with you?"

Harry responded, "Bishop Smith made this assignment. He told us that in *special situations* we can have two teachers or two priests assigned as companions to teach another young man, and then report directly back to him. It's all done under his direct supervision. In fact, the bishop is officially our *third companion* if we ever need any help."

The bishop asked, "Can I ask what the special situation is in this case?"

President Mann answered, "Sure. We have a boy in our quorum with non-member parents. He comes to church once in a while, so the bishop assigned me and my counselor to home teach him. Most of the time we visit him in his home, but sometimes we invite him to one of our homes instead. Sometimes we give him a lesson, but the bishop really just wants us to make sure that he feels like he is part of the quorum. We hang out and talk, ask how he's doing, find out what we should pray for, and we always make sure to invite him to all our activities."

Then Harry added, "We also go with him when he meets with the missionaries."

Bishop Stephens exclaimed, "Wait! I thought you were talking about a boy that was a member of the Church."

Harry laughed and said, "Nope. This is a friend from school that my first counselor invited to church. He liked it and wanted to keep coming. We invited him to listen to the discussions, and he said he would. His parents just gave him permission to be baptized. They're even thinking about listening to the missionaries, too. It's all pretty cool."

Bishop Stephens just shook his head in disbelief. He said, "President, I am so impressed with you and your quorum, and what you are doing. Thanks for your great example. I just have one more question for you. The purpose of Aaronic Priesthood is to help prepare you for more responsibility in the future. How do you think home teaching is helping your quorum members prepare for the rest of their lives?"

President Mann gave that question a little thought and then said, "I think one thing it has done is prepare me to be a missionary. I'm much more confident about teaching and sharing the Gospel with others now.

"Home teaching is also helping us learn how important it is to serve other people. Each of our quorum members has matured a little since we have started learning how to serve our families."

After one more little pause to think, he finally said, "And I would say the most important thing I've learned this last year is that if you will serve and pray for the people you home teach, you will start to love them like your own family."

At first, all that Bishop Stephens could say was, "Wow!" Then he thanked President Mann for teaching him about the role of a quorum president.

He then said, "Do you mind if I call you and set up another time to meet and talk? Maybe I could bring my teacher's quorum president with me. Would you mind?" The bishop was not just asking, he was nearly pleading.

President Mann was excited that he could help and said, "Anytime! My bishop told me to bear my testimony to anyone who would listen, especially about home teaching! He always says that's one of the most important things we do as a priesthood holder. I'll talk to you whenever you want."

And with that, the meeting was over.

NOTES FROM AARONIC PRIESTHOOD:

1. Home teaching is a Priesthood Duty to God.
2. Teach the Aaronic Priesthood quorums the importance of home teaching and how to do it the Lord's way in lessons and by example.
3. Empower Aaronic Priesthood quorum presidents to use the keys and authority that Heavenly Father has given them.
4. Have a Home Teaching Moment before the priesthood lesson and allow the young men to ascertain service needs of the families assigned to quorum members, to bear testimony, and to reinforce the importance of home teaching as their priesthood duty.
5. Remind them the Home Teaching Moment is not a place to divulge confidential or personal information.
6. Enable the presidency to hold regular (not necessarily monthly) stewardship and Home Teaching Interviews similar to the adult HTI.
7. Choose monthly service projects based on needs of the quorum home teaching assignments.
8. In special circumstances, and under the direct supervision of the bishop, teachers and priests can be assigned with other quorum members to home teach young peers with unique needs.

Chapter 8

The Relief Society President

"Let us commit to effective visiting teaching. We can provide temporal and spiritual nourishment. We can and should offer understanding and be able to teach doctrine. We can relieve spiritual hunger and feed the sheep. Feeding the sheep might mean strengthening and nourishing the new members, the less active, or even the fully active members."[18]
Sister Silvia H. Allred

There were just a couple of people left on his list to visit with. One of them was Bishop Smith's Relief Society president. Sister Jensen was more than willing to meet with Bishop Stephens, but insisted on meeting him in his office at church to make it easier on him. The bishop could tell she was aware of the load that a bishop carries.

When the bishop's executive secretary showed Sister Jensen into his office, she immediately reminded him of his own mother. She was an older woman, maybe 70 years old and tiny in stature, but her personality filled the room. She was happy, friendly and extremely complimentary. She immediately made you feel good about yourself.

Bishop Stephens thanked his secretary and invited Sister Jensen to have a seat. The first thing she did was thank the bishop for the opportunity to talk to him.

---

[18] In Conference Report, Oct. 2007, *Feed My Sheep*, Silvia H. Allred,

He said, "Not at all Sister Jensen, thank you for coming to meet with me. I am very impressed with your ward and its leadership. You have done remarkable things in the Mountain Ridge Ward. Your bishop told me that I should meet with you to get a better understanding of what makes your ward so special."

Sister Jensen responded, "The members make it special. They do all the hard work."

She continued quickly, "When the bishop extended The Challenge, he asked all the home and visiting teachers to pray each day for the families they were assigned to.

"As you know, visiting teaching is a little different. The sisters are allowed to make a phone contact from time to time in place of actually visiting the home of their assigned sister, especially if there are issues that make it too difficult to meet together. But a visit is always preferred, and we ask our sisters to do everything in their power to make a personal visit as a companionship."

The bishop nodded, acknowledging that fact.

She quickly went on, "When we first implemented The Challenge, our presidency was thrilled that the sisters embraced it so quickly. We immediately began to see big results."

"What kind of results did you see?" asked the new bishop.

Sister Jensen looked almost excited to explain the benefits they had seen in their ward. She said, "Well, first of all, as the home and visiting teaching improved, so did the Sacrament Meeting attendance. That was a big thing for us. We climbed from 60% attendance in Sacrament Meeting to over 80% attendance!

"All we were doing differently was home and visiting teaching. Of course, our teaching *experience* had changed dramatically, and that was the most important part. We were now praying for our families, serving them, and loving them in a way we hadn't imagined before. When you are doing those things, you seek out those people at church, and hug them and tell them you're glad to see them." She looked at the bishop, smiled and said, "If you can't tell, I'm a hugger!"

He smiled back and said, "I can imagine. So you say meeting attendance went up? That's very interesting…"

Sister Jensen replied, "How could it not go up? The reason most of the less active members of the ward had quit coming was because they didn't feel like they connected with anyone. They would come, and there were times nobody even said hello to them, let alone give them a hug. When your testimony isn't as strong as it needs to be, sometimes you need a friend to keep you coming back each week.

"President Gordon B. Hinckley said, 'Everyone needs a friend, a responsibility, and nurturing with the good word of God.'[19] Members need all three of those things, and I think a friend is one of the most important things on that list, especially for the women. We sisters don't have much of a problem with our testimonies, but we really need to feel loved by someone.

---

[19] In Conference Report, Apr 1997, *Converts and Young Men*, President Gordon B. Hinckley

"Think about how inspired this program is. Every sister has a visiting teaching companion, two visiting teachers that are assigned to visit her, a couple of sisters that she is assigned to visit, and two home teachers. Therefore, every sister in the ward potentially has at least seven built-in friends. The Lord is providing us with a wonderful opportunity to get to know and care for one another," she said with a smile from ear to ear.

"As we started visiting the less active members and showing them an increase of love and concern, rather than just teaching them a lesson, their hearts started to soften. The sisters started sharing their concerns, frustrations, doubts and stumbling blocks. Their visiting teachers were then able to address those issues through prayer, testimony, example, and yes, even in lessons they would give. Very quickly, we started seeing whole families return to Sacrament Meeting. It was wonderful! They were greeted by both of their visiting teachers and both of their home teachers. Can you imagine how they must have felt? Instead of being embarrassed or nervous to return, they felt like they hadn't missed a day. It was a smooth transition, because they had people who were there to greet them and who were genuinely excited to see them."

Bishop Stephens said with a faux frown, "I wish people would greet me with excitement at church."

Sister Jensen jumped on that comment, "We all do! It's nice to feel appreciated. As home and visiting teachers, we should be glad to see our families at church, and we should let them know it, too!"

Bishop Stephens responded, "I would like to see more of that. Sometimes, the little cliques in a ward don't make it easy for the sisters with only a few friends."

"Bishop!" She exclaimed with excitement, "That's another big benefit. All that cliquey behavior has almost completely evaporated in our ward. Sure, we have groups of friends that have similar interests and family experiences, but our ward is a lot more inclusive now. Most of the women have become great friends with the sisters they are assigned to. They have invited their visiting teaching sisters to lunch, over for Family Home Evening, and some sit together at church.

"I have a great example of what I am talking about. A couple of years ago, we assigned a young mother in the ward to visit teach an elderly woman that had become so ill and weak that she wouldn't leave the house. After a while, it was clear to the woman's husband that he could trust and confide in his wife's visiting teacher.

"One day he went over to the younger woman's home and told her that his wife had given up. He said that she wouldn't do any of the exercises that the doctors wanted her to do, and he could tell that she had lost her desire to keep living. Her young visiting teacher defiantly proclaimed, 'She's not allowed to give up!'

"The visiting teacher then set up a daily appointment with her older friend to go walking together. Every day, Bishop! That's love.

"At first it was just to the mail box and back, and then to the end of the street. The last time I saw them, they were walking around the whole block. These two sisters, decades apart in age, have a love for one another like I have never seen before outside the bonds of family. It truly is a remarkable result of home ministering as the Savior would."

Bishop Stephens then asked, "Are there any lingering struggles that you have in your ward? Surely, life isn't perfect yet, is it?" asked Bishop Stephens.

"Of course not. Our ward still struggles in areas, but we're human. We are always going to need to improve. It's funny, the very first time we achieved 100% home teaching and 100% visiting teaching in the same month, our bishop thanked and congratulated us for hitting that milestone, but in the very next breath, he said something like, 'Now that everyone is being visited, let's take it to the next level and really work on the quality of our visits. In our prayers tonight, let's all ask Heavenly Father if there is anything regarding our stewardship that we can do a little better.'"

> *"You can't minister the way the Savior wants you to without making the visit first."*

Bishop Stephens, feeling like he knew Bishop Smith pretty well by now, just smiled and said, "I can see him saying that."

Sister Jensen smiled back and said, "Bishop Smith could tell that some people still felt like reaching 100% was the end-goal, so he simply wanted to remind us that visiting 100% of the homes was only the first step."

Then she added, "The bishop always says, 'Home ministering is never done. The visit is just the minimum requirement of your duty and obligation. You can't minister the way the Savior wants you to without making the visit first.'"

Bishop Stephens had heard that statement before and it made perfect sense that a visit was only the first priority, and ministering was the real goal.

"I'm starting to really like your bishop," he said to the always-happy Relief Society president.

She enthusiastically shot back, "You should! He really cares about the members of our ward. Unfortunately, there were a few people that didn't appreciate his invitation to continue to improve our performance. In fact, after that meeting I heard a couple of men talking to each other in the hall, complaining about the new challenge. I interrupted them and told them the bishop loved them so much that he was willing to be unpopular and ask them to do hard things, just like any good parent would do for a child that they love. I received a couple of embarrassed looks from those two brethren, but they needed to know an old woman like me was going to follow the bishop's counsel. I know Heavenly Father wants me to improve every day, personally and spiritually."

Then Sister Jensen looked at the clock and said, "I'll just share one more thought with you before I go. As you can imagine, quality home and visiting teaching is critical for newly converted members. They need to know, from the very first day, that the Lord loves them. They need to know they have a support system as they try to navigate around a brand new way of life. And finally, they need to know that no matter how tough life gets, they aren't alone, and that they have friends that will help them through any challenge or trial.

"I have seen new members fall away due to a lack of help and attention. They felt very supported and loved throughout the investigator stage, but once they got baptized and their missionaries moved on, they were left to figure things out for themselves. New members need to be nurtured and shepherded throughout their lives, and in reality, so do the rest of us that have been lifelong members! We're all in need of nurturing, just like President Hinckley said.

"That's why I like this emphasis on shepherding the whole flock the way the Lord would do it. If you home or visit teach a lifelong member with the same attention and love that you would show a newly baptized member, then you will see the same type of continuous growth and conversion. It is a marvelous way to care for the ward."

After their time together, as Sister Jensen was walking out of the bishop's office, she turned around and asked, "Did Bishop Smith tell you his story about Elder Walters?"

"No, he didn't. Why?" he asked.

"Oh, that's my favorite story. When you see him again, you need to ask about Elder Walters."

NOTES FROM RELIEF SOCIETY:

1. Even though the Handbook allows Visiting Teaching to be done with a phone call when needed, a visit in the home is always preferred. A phone call should be the exception, not the rule.

2. Women need friends!

3. Just like home teaching, 100% visiting teaching is not the end-goal. You can't minister the way the Savior wants you to without visiting the home.

4. We should ask Heavenly Father what more we can do every day.

5. Bishops and ward leaders invite their flocks to do hard things, because they love them and want them to continue to grow and improve spiritually.

6. Home and visiting teaching is vital in the retention process of new members, as well as the reactivation process of less-active members.

7. Home and visiting teaching helps any member—both new and lifelong—experience continual growth and conversion and feel the Lord's love.

Chapter 9

The Home Minister

"Help me find thy lambs that wander, Help me bring them
to thy keep, Teach me Lord, to be a shepherd;
Father, help me feed thy sheep."[20]
Help Me Teach with Inspiration; Hymn 281, verse 4

Brother Michaels was the last person on the list of suggested visits from Bishop Smith. Brother Michaels was listed as a "Home Minister" on the list, and Bishop Stephens thought that was interesting. He was really looking forward to see what wisdom would flow from this interview.

This time however, unlike the other interviews, Brother Michaels wasn't expecting a phone call. Once Bishop Stephens had explained his visits with the Mountain Ridge Ward leadership, Brother Michaels was glad to help, although he was surprised that he had been chosen from among all the other fine examples in his ward. He was happy the bishop thought he had something to contribute.

When the two men met, Bishop Stephens took control of the interview. He told Brother Michaels what he had learned so far and asked if there was anything more he could add to help the new bishop implement this method of Home Teaching in his own ward.

---

[20] *Help Me Teach With Inspiration*, Hymns (Salt Lake City: The Church of Jesus Christ of Latter-day Saints, 1985) no. 281

Brother Michaels thought about it for a few seconds and said, "It's only been the last few years, since The Challenge, that I feel I've really understood what home teaching is and what it can do to nurture and strengthen families and individuals. I've caught the vision of home teaching now, and I understand what the Lord expects from me as a minister in the home."

He pulled out his scriptures and said, "In the Book of Mosiah it says we should be willing to '*bear one another's burdens, that they may be light;...mourn with those that mourn;... comfort those that stand in need of comfort, and...stand as witnesses of God at all times and in all things, and in all places...*'"[21]

Then Brother Michaels said, "This is our responsibility as members of the Church. This is what home teaching is to me now: Serving God by caring for and ministering to the needs of my own family and the families I home teach. That is why we need to pray about each family, to receive inspiration for each individual, and to know how best to care for them and help them 'come unto Christ.'[22] Let me give you an example.

"One of the people I have been assigned to shepherd is a widow. She's been very lonely since the death of her husband, and she has had many struggles and challenges. When my companion and I go to her home, sometimes all is well in the home and we simply give the lesson that's assigned. There are times she needs a blessing of comfort, direction or peace. On

---

[21] Book of Mormon - Another Testament of Jesus Christ, Mosiah 18:8-10

[22] Doctrine and Covenants 20:59

other visits, we discern very quickly that she just needs to talk. We are also in touch with her several times each month by phone, and we always make sure that we find her at church and give her a hug and let her know that we love her. She feels very cared for and knows that we are aware of her concerns."

Then he said, "I have three other families that I home teach with my son."

Bishop Stephens picked up on that and asked, "So you have two different companions?"

Brother Michaels replied, "There have been times when I've had *three different companions*. One time I was paired with my wife to teach a single sister, I taught another family with my son, and I was also paired with an Elder for a third family. We are assigned by inspiration, so if Heavenly Father knows that a family—or a single sister—needs the experience of two high priests, a husband and wife, or a father and son, we will get assigned accordingly.

"Based on the feedback our bishop receives from the Home Teaching Interviews, he and the quorum leaders are able to make educated and inspired adjustments to companionships, as needed, so each family has the best possible home ministers for their specific needs. The bishop always says, *'Information is inspiration,'* and I would agree.

"My son is able to go with me to the other three families that I currently teach. One is a traditional family with a husband, wife and three kids, and another is a retired elderly couple. The last family is a single mom with three kids, and one of them is on a mission. Each have their own issues, as we all do, but none that require a special assignment."

"Wow! You're a model home teacher," said the bishop.

Brother Michaels guffawed. "I am far from the model home teacher. When the bishop initially issued The Challenge, I actually *refused* to home teach. The bishop had to call me in and explain the purpose of the home teaching program, and how I was needed by the families that I was assigned to. He made it perfectly clear I was assigned by the Lord, not him. He said Heavenly Father had given me specific talents and gifts, and now He needed me to use those gifts to minister to my assigned families. The bishop also said that he was certain that they would respond to no other home teacher as well as they would respond to me. He told me he would release me from all my other callings, if needed, to ensure I had enough time to magnify this one, because it was by far the most important."

Bishop Stephens had heard this story before, but he was completely caught off guard hearing it come from this great home teacher. Then he hesitantly asked Brother Michaels if there was a Brother Jones in the ward or if President Baugh had actually disguised Brother Michaels' name when he related a similar story. Brother Michaels laughed out loud and confirmed that he was indeed the hold-out home teacher in the story.

Bishop Stephens looked at him and said, "I assure you that President Baugh had nothing but high praise for the reformed home teacher in that story."

"Thanks," said Brother Michaels. "I fully sustain my leaders. The bishop did what he needed to do, and it changed my whole paradigm of home teaching and helped me develop a testimony of the principle of shepherding the Lord's flock.

"Bishop Smith cared enough about me, and the families I was assigned to home teach, that he did the hard thing by calling me in and testifying of the importance of this work. I have never had a bishop care enough before to tell me to repent for being a lousy home teacher—my words, not his. My other bishops have just put up with me, but not Bishop Smith. He saw me neglecting one of my primary responsibilities as a priesthood holder, and lovingly helped me understand that I needed to repent and change the way I looked at home teaching, as much for myself, as for the families to whom I was assigned. The bishop was a true example of 'standing as a witness.'

"After that experience, I think I actually understood how Peter felt when the resurrected Savior came back and caught the apostles fishing instead of feeding His flock. Jesus asked Peter three times if he loved Him. Over and over he answered that he did love the Lord, but probably with less confidence each time he was asked. Three times Peter declared his love for the Lord, and three times he was commanded to 'Feed my sheep.'[23] By the end of Peter's interview, I think he was pretty resolved to feed the Lord's sheep. I assure you, at the end of my interview with the bishop, I was also extremely resolved to *feed the sheep.*"

---

[23] John 21:15-17

With great humility, Brother Michaels admitted, "I will always be grateful that my bishop had the *courage* to remind me of the oath and covenant that I had made."

"That is remarkable," said Bishop Stephens. "Thank you for sharing such a personal story."

"It's my pleasure. I feel it's my duty to bear my testimony of home teaching. If there is another priesthood holder in your ward that needs encouragement, send him my way."

Smiling, he responded, "I'll keep that in mind!"

Then Brother Michaels got very serious and said, "I'm not kidding. We all need help at times. There's a great analogy of home ministering found in a war story in the Book of Mormon.

"During one battle, every Stripling Warrior was injured, some to the point that they fainted from so many wounds. After the battle, the wounded warriors that could still walk were commanded to go back into the battlefield, find their brethren that were critically wounded, and attend to their injuries.[24]

"Bishop, *we are all wounded warriors*—some, more than others. But, those of us who are still standing are commanded to go into the battlefield and rescue and succor our brothers and sisters. We all need to be ministered to at some point."

Bishop Stephens assured Brother Michaels that he would indeed use him as a resource in the future and thanked him for the offer. The two new friends then bid each other a good evening.

---

[24] Book of Mormon - Another Testament of Jesus Christ, Alma 57:19-27

NOTES FROM HOME MINISTER:

1. Home teaching is much more than the lesson. It's bearing one another's burdens, giving comfort and standing as a witness, at all times.

2. Companionships are prayerfully considered and assigned based on the needs of the family members.

3. Bishops should get all the information they can from quorum leaders' Home Teaching Interviews so they can make educated and inspired decisions about companionships.

4. Inspiration comes from information!

5. It's okay to mix and match companionships to best suit the needs of each family.

6. Sometimes a Personal Priesthood Interview is needed with a home teacher that is not fully committed, to remind him that diligent home teaching is a priesthood requirement—just like tithing or priesthood meeting attendance is a requirement. Personally bear your testimony, and teach the importance of the calling.

Chapter 10

The Bishop (Part 2)

"...Oh, that all the brethren of the Church would catch
that vision of home teaching!"[25]
President Ezra Taft Benson

After a very enlightening journey with the leadership of the
Mountain Ridge Ward, Bishop Stephens was eager to meet with
Bishop Smith again and discuss what he had learned.

The two greeted each other and then Bishop Smith asked,
"Well, what do you think?"

Bishop Stephens looked at his mentor and then said
sincerely, "After all these years, I think I finally understand what
is expected of me as a priesthood holder. Thank you."

The veteran bishop smiled and replied, "I'm glad we could
help. Now that you've caught the vision of *home ministering*, you
need to apply what you know, or this was all for nothing. Lots
of other leaders have seen what we're doing, but many have
chosen not to act on it. It's just human nature, unfortunately, to
take the path of least resistance.

"It is similar to someone receiving the missionary lessons and
feeling the Spirit tell them that it's true, yet when it comes right
down to actually doing something about it, they decide that it's
just too hard to change.

---

[25] In Conference Report, Apr. 1987, *To the Home Teachers of the Church*,
President Ezra Taft Benson

"There are also some bishops who just don't see the potential of home and visiting teaching beyond delivering a lesson from a magazine. When they look at this program with the paradigm of *teaching*, it's hard for them to visualize how blessed the members of their wards can be with home ministers assigned to each family.

"Additionally, there's nothing easy about getting an entire ward to work harder at something they think they're already doing well. The biggest challenge for us was getting the ward members to look at home and visiting teaching differently, and to minister in the homes a little better. To *pray daily* for each of their families by name, and to listen to Heavenly Father's direction when He tells them how they can better serve their families. It wasn't easy, but once they tried it, they were hooked."

Bishop Stephens nodded thoughtfully, and after letting that sink in for a moment he asked, "I can see how this can work in an area like ours, where we don't have to travel more than an hour to visit any family in our ward, but how does this work in a larger geographical area?"

Bishop Smith answered, "Exactly the same way. The more a ward is spread out, the more important it is to home minister.

"Now of course, there are some wards that have lower activity levels, and their resources to home and visit teach effectively are stretched pretty thin. But that doesn't change the Lord's mandate to visit the home of each member.

"As the Handbook says, bishops and quorum leaders may need to make adjustments from time to time. They may need to concentrate most of their efforts on the less-active and new members occasionally, but the Handbook also says that should happen only 'temporarily.'[26] There may be times that the quorums and Relief Society need to collaborate and pair a husband and wife team together to do home and visiting teaching at the same time. In extreme cases and where distance is a real problem, like Alaska, or someplace else where members are spread out geographically, home teachers may need to make a phone call or video-chat with a family to see how they're doing and what they can pray for. Technology has come a long way, and we have lots of new options to stay connected to one another. If we quit looking at home and visiting teaching as just a lesson from a magazine, we will find that there are many ways to *minister* to the needs of the families and individuals we are assigned to visit.

> "...if we quit looking at home teaching as just a sit-down-lesson, we will find that there are lots of ways to 'minister' to the needs of the families..."

"But in the end, we are accountable to Heavenly Father for this stewardship. He knows if we are doing all that we can do, and He will tell us if we need to do more. We just need to listen."

---

[26] *Handbook 2: Administering in the Church;* (Salt Lake City, The Church of Jesus Christ of Latter-day Saints, 2010). p. 44 - Section 7.4.3

Then Bishop Smith added, "President Hinckley always told us 'Do your very, very best,'[27] and 'Try a little harder to be a little better.'[28] By now, you probably know that I subscribe to that philosophy. If we do our *very, very* best, we will bless a lot of people through home ministering."

"But Bishop…" the veteran waited until Bishop Stephens was looking right into his eyes.

"Bishop, you must remember, most of the things we do in our ward—especially with regard to home ministering—are not spelled out in the Handbook. It only gives us the outline, and we are to use the Holy Ghost to fill in the blanks for our own stewardships. Our way may not be your way. Be prayerful and the Lord will tell you how you should implement the shepherding process in your own ward."

Bishop Stephens smiled and nodded. Then he remembered what Sister Jensen had said, and he asked, "Can you tell me about Elder Walters? Sister Jensen said it was one of her favorite stories."

Bishop Smith leaned back in his chair, smiled and said, "Well, I have to admit, it's my favorite story, too. The experience actually changed my life."

Bishop Smith slowly swung his chair to the side to face the only window in his office. He stared out that window for a long

---

[27] In Conference Report, Apr. 1999, *Find the Lambs, Feed the Sheep*, President Gordon B. Hinckley

[28] In Conference Report, Apr. 1995, *We Have a Work To Do*, President Gordon B. Hinckley

moment, as if he was transporting himself back in time. Then he began...

"I actually grew up in a home with inactive parents who eventually divorced. Understandably, I became a very unhappy kid with a big chip on my shoulder. Luckily, I had some really good friends who were active members of the Church. They consistently invited me to church and kept close tabs on me as we were growing up. But after graduation, when they all began leaving for college and missions, I started to fade away from the Church again. I had never actually gained a real testimony for myself, and without friends, there just wasn't anything keeping me coming back. I didn't have any home teachers assigned to me, so there was nobody encouraging me to keep attending.

"My very inspired bishop saw me slipping away, and called me in for an interview. That's when he challenged me to serve a mission. I actually laughed at him and said, 'Not me! A mission is not for me.' Thank goodness he wouldn't accept my answer and asked me to go home and think about it for a few weeks.

"Well, the Lord didn't give me a *few weeks*. He went to work on me immediately, and within just a couple of days, I had a profound spiritual experience that confirmed that I needed to serve a mission. So to my own amazement, I returned to the bishop and started the paperwork.

"As you can imagine though, not long after I got into the mission field, my brand-new testimony was put to the test. It could only carry me so far, and I began struggling to conform. One of my first companions told the mission president that I had a big chip on my shoulder and needed an attitude adjustment—which was true!" He looked at Bishop Stephens, smiled and shrugged, and then continued.

"When news of my transfer arrived, so did the warnings. Before I could even get my bags packed, the missionaries in my district offered their condolences and gave me advance warning of all the failings of Elder Walters, my companion-to-be. Of course, those elders had never actually met Elder Walters, nonetheless I foolishly considered them to be completely reliable sources. So, without ever meeting my new companion, I already disliked him.

"Several hours later, I arrived in a beautiful little town on the coast of Spain. That's when I first saw my six-foot-five missionary companion, lumbering down the sidewalk toward me. Without even hearing him say a word, I immediately felt threatened, and my wall went up. Unjustifiably, I decided at that very moment that all of the stories about him were true.

"Within a day, my dislike for him had turned to *loathing* for the way he walked, the way he talked, and even the way he chewed his food. There was nothing that I found redeeming about Elder Walters, and it didn't take him long to sense it. Keep in mind, this poor elder had done nothing wrong, but as could be expected from my bad behavior, he was starting to feel the same way about me." Bishop Smith was shaking his head, clearly disappointed in the story he was telling about himself.

"On the third day I was with Elder Walters, the assistants to the mission president came to our apartment under the pretense of doing companion splits. To this day, I still believe the mission president only sent them to determine if we were still alive or if we had beaten each other to death.

"The assistant that I split off with was a very happy, charismatic, red-headed kid. He had a gift of making people feel like they were his best friend, and I immediately felt I could trust him." Bishop Smith was beginning to smile again.

He continued, "So, I told that elder what was going on and begged him for an emergency transfer. I told him that nobody should be subjected to this type of punishment, and I wanted out of this companionship, or I was going home.

"To his credit, the assistant held his ground and told me that I wasn't going anywhere for at least a month. He said that the assignment came by inspiration and that Heavenly Father expected me to serve valiantly while I was there. He added that I couldn't serve well without the Spirit, therefore I better quickly figure out how to love Elder Walters so that the Spirit could return to our companionship.

"I explained that loving Elder Walters was not possible, and even if I wanted to, Elder Walters didn't like me either.

"Then this kid, who was only about a year older than I was, challenged me to do something that changed the way I would eventually live my life, the way I would raise my children, and even the way I would minister to this ward." Bishop Smith then looked at Bishop Stephens and raised his eyebrows as if to ask, *Are you ready for what I'm about to share with you?*

Bishop Stephens gave him an eager nod to prompt him forward.

Bishop Smith smiled and then looked back out the window. He said, "This great young man challenged me to do just one simple thing each day that transformed our companionship of mutual dislike and failure, to a companionship of love that would witness miracles and change lives. His challenge was simple:

"He told me that if I would perform one act of selfless service for my companion—every day—by the end of the month my hate for him would turn to love."

Bishop Smith let that hang in the air for a second and then continued, "He said that if I would shine his shoes, cook him breakfast, make his bed or give any other type of service, including pray for him each day, my heart would begin to change, and I would come to love him."

"Of course," the veteran bishop said sarcastically, "because I knew everything back then, I scoffed and told him that he was nuts. I told him there was no way I could ever love Elder Walters. But eventually, after some encouragement from the young elder, and after realizing that I wasn't getting out of that companionship until the next transfer, I reluctantly accepted his challenge.

"I started praying for Elder Walters that same day, and I continued to do something nice for him for the rest of that month. After a couple of days, it actually became fun. I even started making a game out of it, trying to top what I had done the day before. After about a week, Elder Walters caught on to what I was doing, and it almost became a competition to see who could outdo the other person's last act of service.

"I couldn't believe it, but in just a few days Elder Walters and I were already friends, and I can honestly say that by the end of the month, service had changed my hateful heart. I had actually grown to love Elder Walters, and neither of us wanted to be transferred apart. We still keep in contact to this day."

Bishop Smith was looking at Bishop Stephens now. He then said with a chuckle and a tone of absolute fact, "That wise young assistant changed the course of my life. Not only did his counsel help me find the desire to keep serving my mission and become a better missionary, he inadvertently removed the chip that had been on my shoulder since I was a young child. And the most important thing he did for me—back in that little Spanish town—was reveal the roadmap to true happiness in this life. He showed me that *selfless service leads to Christlike love.*"

Bishop Stephens listened silently, as he took in everything this great man was sharing.

Then Bishop Smith said something that pricked the heart of his new friend. He said, "Bishop, it may already be obvious to you, but I want you to know that even more important than all the practical benefits that are provided to the families through home and visiting teaching, the real spiritual blessings of the service rendered are given to the ones who valiantly perform the service.

"The Lord told us that if we love Him, we should keep His commandments. And what are His commandments?" he asked rhetorically, and then quickly continued. "The first great commandment is to love God, and the second is to love our neighbor. I am convinced that the key to keeping those two commandments is serving those around us. The more you serve someone, the more your love grows for that person. It's as simple as that."

Bishop Stephens was nodding quietly in agreement, so Bishop Smith continued sharing his wisdom. He said, "As you know, service to our spouse is one of the most important things that we can do to transform the romantic love—the feeling that attracted us to one another—into a Christlike love that will endure through the eternities.

"However, there's no promise or guarantee that the people we serve will love us in return, and we can't perform any service with an expectation that they will. But regardless of how they feel about us, we have a promise from our Father, that if we serve His children, *our love for them will continue to grow.*

"For example, a mother can't help loving her child, even if he's been disrespectful and disobedient, simply because of all the service she's given to that child, every-single-day of his life.

"And on a much more eternal level, the Savior loves each of us as a result of the infinite sacrificial service that He rendered on our behalf, through His Atonement, despite our disobedience or our feelings about Him. No matter how far we stray, the Good Shepherd will always love His flock.

"So, as we serve others, *our* hearts change. And as we have been taught, when we are serving His children, we also are serving Him, therefore our love for *Him* will inevitably grow, too. That's how we keep *the two great commandments.*

"Love is what makes our home and visiting teaching so effective in this ward. If our intentions were phony, people would see right though it, and then this whole effort would fail. We have seen miracles in our ward through the home ministering program, because our members genuinely love the families they are assigned to.

"Our home and visiting teachers love their families because they serve them, even if the only service that they give is a daily prayer. Remember, *prayer is service, too.* And the key to sincere and effective home ministering is praying daily for the families we home and visit teach.

> *"Prayer is service, too. The key to sincere and effective home ministering is praying each day for the families we home and visit teach."*

"If every home and visiting teacher throughout the world would pray each day for the families they visit, and then follow the inspiration that will naturally come, it would change their hearts and their efforts, and our wards and stakes would truly begin to feel like Zion."

As Bishop Stephens sat there feeling the Spirit testify of all the truth he had received—and trying to process it all—the veteran bishop leaned forward again and asked, "Bishop, the first day we met, I told you that I had finally figured out the purpose for home ministering—the real reason for the assignments that we receive. Do you remember what I said to you that day?"

Bishop Stephens had received so much new information the last few days that he had to admit that he couldn't remember.

Bishop Smith then pulled out his scriptures and turned to Moroni 7 in the Book of Mormon and began to read:

> "'Wherefore, my beloved brethren, if ye have not charity, ye are nothing, for charity never faileth. Wherefore, cleave unto charity, which is the greatest of all, for all things must fail—
>
> 'But charity is the pure love of Christ, and it endureth forever; and whoso is found possessed of it at the last day, it shall be well with him.
>
> 'Wherefore, my beloved brethren, pray unto the Father with all the energy of heart, that ye may be filled with this love, which he hath bestowed upon all who are true followers of his Son, Jesus Christ; that ye may become the sons of God; that when he shall appear **we shall be like him**, for we shall see him as he is; that we may have this hope; that we may be purified even as he is pure. Amen.'"[29]

---

[29] Book of Mormon - Another Testament of Jesus Christ, Moroni 7:46-48

"Think about that! The one word that describes Jesus Christ best is *Love*. And like the scripture says, if we are to become 'like Him,' we need to develop a Christlike love, or charity.

"Unfortunately, so many members of the Church spend their whole lives stressing about not being adequate—not living up to Heavenly Father's expectations. They don't see a realistic path for themselves to *do all that they need to do* to earn entrance into His presence. But what those people don't understand is that *we are judged by who we have become,* not what we have done."

Then, with incredible passion and sincerity, Bishop Smith asked, "Bishop, is it possible that the real reason that the Good Shepherd has given every adult member of the Church a home or visiting teaching assignment is to provide each of us a simple, effective and proven way to become 'like Him?'"

Bishop Smith then asked another rhetorical question, "And is it also possible that *becoming like Christ* could be as simple as: Repent - Serve like Him - Love like Him - Become like Him? The answer is YES—it's that easy! The Gospel *is* that easy!"

"The change that happens to the truly valiant home or visiting teacher is divinely designed. As they *serve their neighbor* like the Savior would, they begin to *love their neighbor* like the Savior does. When they finally begin to love like Him, they will actually begin to *become* 'like Him.'"

And then without any prompting, the veteran bishop began reciting the following quote from memory:

"'Brethren, home teaching is not just another program. It is the priesthood way of watching over the Saints and accomplishing the mission of the Church. Home teaching is not just an assignment. It is a sacred calling...a program that touches hearts, that changes lives, and that saves souls; a program that has the stamp of approval of our Father in Heaven; a program so vital that, if faithfully followed, it will help to spiritually renew the Church and exalt its individual members and families.'"[30]

Then Bishop Smith smiled, and said with resolve, "Bishop, you'll never know how grateful I am to have been exiled to that little pueblo with Elder Walters, because it was there that I was taught the most important Gospel lesson—*Christlike love comes through selfless service to others.*"

---

[30] In Conference Report, Apr. 1987, *To the Home Teachers of the Church*, President Ezra Taft Benson

MORE NOTES FROM THE BISHOP:

1. Home teachers in wards that cover a larger geographical area have the same mandate to watch over and strengthen their assigned families. In fact, home teaching is even more important in larger wards.

2. At times, bishops and quorum leaders may need to focus more efforts on less-active and new members, but "only temporarily."

3. Home teachers may need to get creative in how they check in with families, ascertain needs, and minister to those needs.

4. "Try a little harder, to be a little better." - President Gordon B. Hinckley

5. We're accountable to God for our stewardship. He knows if we are doing our best and will tell us what more we can do…if we will listen.

6. Christlike love comes from service to the Good Shepherd's flock.

7. Prayer is service, too.

8. The key to sincere and effective home ministering is praying each day for the families we home and visit teach, and then following the inspiration we receive.

9. Is it possible that the real purpose of the Home and Visiting Teaching program is to help the valiant home and visiting teacher *become like the Savior?*

Chapter 11

The Challenge

"The family is the basic unit in the Church Organization. The home teacher is the first line of defense to watch over and strengthen that basic unit. In our priority of time commitments we ought to first watch over and strengthen our own families, and then be good, consistent conscientious home teachers."[31]
Elder L. Tom Perry

The mentor looked at Bishop Stephens and said, "Well, after everything you've heard and seen, would you agree that there's no secret to what we do in this ward? We simply execute the home and visiting teaching programs, and shepherd the flock, the way the Lord intended it to be done."

The new bishop agreed that there were no secrets revealed in his discussions with the ward leaders in Bishop Smith's ward. Bishop Stephens had read Section 20 in the Doctrine and Covenants many times, and he was well aware of the description of home ministering, but he had never seen a ward take it to the level prescribed in the scriptures. Why? He had only two answers: Tradition and Habit.

Bishop Stephens then reluctantly said, "I'm actually a little embarrassed that it's taken me so long to see what these two programs are really all about—how inspired and important they

---

[31] In Conference Report, Oct. 1978, *Home Teaching - A Sacred Calling*, Elder L. Tom Perry

are to the families that I visit, and to my own personal spiritual growth and perfection. I feel like I've just realized that the Mona Lisa was sitting in a cardboard box in my attic. It was there all the time, but I just couldn't see its value."

Bishop Smith then continued, "It's okay! Now that you know—change! Implement these principles in your own stewardship, and issue *The Challenge* to each member in your ward. Invite them to pray everyday for the welfare of their home and visiting teaching families, and to follow the direction that Heavenly Father gives them when the inspiration is received.

"You know, sometimes people come up to me and say, 'I've never heard the Holy Ghost speak to me, or give me direction like that,' and I tell them, 'Sure you have!'

"Then I give them a simple task. I just challenge them, especially the youth, to get down on their knees for their evening prayers with a piece of paper and a pencil, and ask Heavenly Father, 'What is one thing that I can do better tomorrow?'—and then write down the answer.

"I give everyone my personal guarantee that they will feel the Holy Ghost put at least one idea into their head that they can do better the next day—maybe three or four. After they have done that, they need to ask if there is anything they can do better as a home minister and listen for that direction, too.

"As they get used to hearing the promptings, more will come —unless they don't act on that inspiration, of course."

Bishop Smith smiled again and said, "I have a good friend who always says, 'If the Holy Ghost is telling you to do something that you really don't want to do, don't worry about it! Just ignore Him long enough, and that feeling will go away.'"[32]

After a little chuckle the bishop continued, "Of course, it's meant to be a joke, but it's also absolutely true. We must act on inspiration or Heavenly Father will find someone else to accomplish His will. But then the other people will receive the blessings for being obedient—instead of us."

Bishop Stephens had been spiritually filled. He felt blessed to have been educated by such a loving and dedicated servant of the Lord. He felt the same appreciation for Bishop Smith as Bishop Smith had for his long-ago mission assistant.

However, the two bishops seemed to sense at the same time that their conversation was drawing to a close, and it was time to get back to the work of the Lord. Bishop Smith got up from his chair, extended his hand across the desk, and said, "Bishop, it's been a pleasure. You are going to be a great leader. I can tell that you already love your ward enough to ask them to do the hard things."

As the two bishops walked out of the office and into the hall, Bishop Smith couldn't resist sharing one more piece of advice. He said, "Bishop, if we, as the shepherds of the flock, are going to magnify our callings, we will need to ask our ward members to raise the bar from time to time, and do more. That's not how we win the Mr. Popularity award, but that's our job.

---

[32] Quote by Steven E. Garner

"My daughter's mission president always told his missionaries, 'Be bold, be clear and be quiet.'[33]

"I've always liked the '*be quiet*' part. Sometimes, after we invite our members to do something that's outside their comfort zones, we feel like we need to justify or make excuses for what we are asking them to do. Don't ever be shy about inviting people to do what the Lord wants them to do. It's our job.

"But after we tell our ward members what the Holy Ghost wants us to reveal to them, we need to 'be quiet,' and let Him confirm in their hearts that it is a *Gospel truth*. At that point, they need to choose for themselves whether they will follow the Good Shepherd or wander off from His flock and get lost.

"Now, go back to your ward, and 'be bold, be clear and be quiet' and you will see hearts changed and miracles happen. I promise."

And he did.

---

[33] Quoted by President Ronald L. Craven - North Carolina, Charlotte Mission (2012-15) (Original quote by Elder W. Craig Zwick)

Author's Note to the Brethren of the Church

Over 20 years ago, I was called to serve as an elders quorum president. Prior to receiving my calling, our Area Authority Seventy promised the stake presidency that if they could get the quorum presidencies to commit to hold monthly Home Teaching Interviews, the home teaching in the stake would double. Our home teaching was averaging 40% at the time. With the new calling and mandate, my presidency began holding our monthly interviews.

Initially there was a little resistance from the quorum, but during the first interview with each companionship we explained the purpose, the goal, and the doctrine behind what we were doing. We expressed our love for each of the elders and the families they were teaching, and told them that we had confidence they would rise to the challenge. And rise, they did! As promised by the inspired General Authority, within two months our home teaching visits climbed from 40% to 85%, and we never looked back. It was clear that the Home Teaching Interviews made the difference.

As the home and visiting teachers get used to being accountable for reporting the welfare status of their families, rather than just saying, "I did it," the visits will be more meaningful in every home.

In my next ward we made improvements to the program, and we experienced all the results spoken of in this book.

Although the story in this book is fictional, almost all of the examples actually occurred.

I have seen the challenges and the blessings of ministering to the flock the way the Savior wants us to. There are definitely growing pains at first, but if the home ministers create the following habits, the visits will become more meaningful, and the teacher/family relationship will blossom and mature to the point that almost all concerns and issues will be handled through the shepherding channels:

- Ask each family what you should be praying for as a companionship and in your personal prayers
- Pray everyday about those concerns or needs, also asking for revelation regarding how to better serve the family
- Do what you can to meet the family's needs, and then use your quorum resources, if necessary, to make up for any lack in your own ability to meet those needs
- Begin giving detailed reports each month on the welfare of each family, rather than just saying, "I did it," or "It's all done."

Remember, this is not an optional program. This is a commandment, which we have made a covenant to keep. We must never get complacent in our efforts to magnify our priesthood as home ministers. Average is not good enough! The Savior desires valiant, Ammon-like shepherds.

Captain Moroni is another great example from the Book of Mormon of the type of priesthood holders we should be.

The following was said about Moroni:

> *"And Moroni was a strong and a mighty man; he was a man of a perfect understanding;*
> *"...a man who did labor exceedingly for the welfare and safety of his people.*
> *"Yea, and he was a man who was firm in the faith of Christ, and he had sworn with an oath to defend his people, his rights, and his country, and his religion, even to the loss of his blood...*
> *"Yea, verily, verily I say unto you, if all men had been, and were, and ever would be, like unto Moroni, behold, the very powers of hell would have been shaken forever; yea, the devil would never have power over the hearts of the children of men." Alma 48:11-13; 17*

Brethren, you have also sworn an oath to "labor exceedingly for the welfare and safety of *your* people." You have the ability, if cultivated, to be "like unto Moroni" in your shepherding stewardships, and if you do, "the very powers of hell" will shake, and the devil will lose his power over the "hearts of the children" that you minister to.

And if we magnify the Oath and Covenant of the Priesthood, we will be rewarded with the greatest of gifts, even an inheritance of "all that our Father hath."[34]

I testify that home and visiting teaching is the Good Shepherd's method of caring for His flock and protecting families from Satan's grasp. It will bless the lives of those that teach, and those that are taught, as love and trust between the shepherd and the lamb are natural consequences.

I also testify that faithful home and visiting teachers will come to know the Savior better as they minister the way He would minister, serve the way He would serve, and care the way He would care. Home and visiting teaching callings are actually self-improvement gifts from the Lord. If we will just implement what is taught in the scriptures, and by modern-day prophets, this program will help each of us obtain the promise of being filled with charity and becoming like Him.

May the Lord bless and guide you in your efforts to shepherd the portion of His flock that you have been entrusted with. Happy home ministering!

---

[34] Doctrine & Covenants 84:38

Talks on Home and Visiting Teaching

To the Home Teachers of the Church
President Ezra Taft Benson
April 1987 General Conference

True Shepherds
President Thomas S. Monson
October 2013 General Conference

Home Teaching - A Sacred Calling
Elder L. Tom Perry
October 1978 General Conference

Feed My Sheep
Sister Silvia H. Allred
October 2007 General Conference

Home Teachers—Watchmen Over the Church
James A. Cullimore
October 1972 General Conference

The Saints Securely Dwell
Elder Boyd K. Packer
October 1972 General Conference

About the Author

Steve Webber lives in Cedar Hills, Utah, with his wife, Jana. They are the parents of five amazing children; four daughters and a son.

Among other callings, Steve has served as young mens president, elders quorum president, high priest group leader, bishop and home teacher, giving him a unique perspective on the effect that valiant home ministers can have on the flock of the Good Shepherd.

Steve served an LDS mission in the Spain, Barcelona mission, and later graduated from Brigham Young University in Business Management. He owns Timpanogos Media, LLC.

Ordering Information for Wards and Stakes

The purpose of *Shepherds of the Flock* is to help home and visiting teachers catch the vision of the true purpose and potential of their calling. After sharing the manuscript with local ward and stake leaders, and receiving their passionate feedback, it became clear to the author that the principles taught in this book had the potential to create a widespread groundswell of enthusiasm for home ministering.

This effort is about helping members understand how to shepherd the flock, thus the price point on this book has been kept as low as possible. However, to help deliver the message to an even larger audience, the author is providing group/bulk discounts (up to 40% off the cover price) for ward and stake leaders who want to make *Shepherds of the Flock* available to the members in their area.

For quotes on orders of 25 books or more, contact the author directly at:

1-801-369-3029
Steve@TimpMedia.com
www.ShepherdsOfTheFlock.com

61824329R00074

Made in the USA
Lexington, KY
21 March 2017